Maria Runciman, L.C.S.W.
Diplomate In Clinical Social Work
P.O. Box 6383
Oxnard, Califiornia 93031-6383

Our Share of Night,
Our Share of Morning

Nancy Fuchs

Our Share of Night, Our Share of Morning

*Parenting As a
Spiritual Journey*

HarperSanFrancisco
An Imprint of HarperCollins*Publishers*

HarperSanFrancisco and the author, in association with The Basic Foundation, a not-for-profit organization whose primary mission is reforestation, will facilitate the planting of two trees for every one tree used in the manufacture of this book.

A TREE CLAUSE BOOK

HarperCollins Web Site: http://www.harpercollins.com
HarperCollins®, 📖®, HarperSanFrancisco™, and A TREE CLAUSE BOOK®
are trademarks of HarperCollins Publishers, Inc.

FIRST EDITION

Library of Congress Cataloging-in-Publication Data
Fuchs, Nancy.
Our share of night, our share of morning : parenting as a
spiritual journey / Nancy Fuchs. — 1st ed.
ISBN 0-06-251288-9 (cloth)
ISBN 0-06-251285-4 (pbk.)
1. Parenting—Religious life.   2. Parenting—Religious aspects.
3. Spiritual life.   4. Fuchs, Nancy.   I. Title.
BL625.8.F83   1996
291.4'4—dc20   95-49539

96 97 98 99 00 ❖HAD 10 9 8 7 6 5 4 3 2 1

: *To Dorothy Traylor,*
who has been a spiritual teacher to our family

: *Our share of night to bear,*
  Our share of morning,
  Our blank in bliss to fill,
  Our blank in scorning.

  Here a star, and there a star,
  Some lose their way.
  Here a mist, and there a mist,
  Afterwards—day!

EMILY DICKINSON

Contents

Acknowledgments

This book would not exist without the honesty and generosity of the more than one hundred parents whom I interviewed. In order to protect their confidentiality, I have disguised their identities, changing many details and at times creating composite stories. However, when I quote a personal friend directly (as in "My friend Judy said . . . "), this is a real remark by a real person, and his or her actual name is used.

I am grateful to the many people who read all or parts of this manuscript: Marjorie Bosk, Rabbi Sue Levi Elwell, Beverly Fuchs, Paula Fuchs, Victor Fuchs, Frances Kreimer, Rabbi Joy Levitt, Rachelle Marshall, Maria Papacastaki, Emilie Passow, Debbie Rogow, Marian Sandmaier, Rabbi Reena Spicehandler, and special thanks to Judy Petsonk. I also thank my rabbinical students who listened to portions of the book at an early stage and to Arthur Samuelson of Schocken and Susan Worst of Beacon who encouraged me in the beginning. My agent, Anne Edelstein, was a perfect choice, whose advice was always just right. Working with HarperSanFrancisco, I benefited greatly from the skill and dedication of my editor, John Loudon, assistant editor Karen Levine, and copy editor Nancy Palmer Jones.

The president and the dean of the Reconstructionist Rabbinical College, Rabbi David Teutsch and Rabbi Jacob Staub, have been exceptionally supportive of this endeavor.

I thank my daughters whom I have tried to teach two lessons: be a mensch and have fun. They have tried to teach me the same. I am also grateful to my parents for many gifts, including raising me within Reconstructionist Judaism, a community that continues to nurture me on my own journey.

Most of all, I would like to thank my husband, Seth Kreimer, for tremendous help on many fronts—from convincing me not to quit in the beginning to editing drafts of the manuscript and coming up with the title. Seth has stuck by me through our share of night and our share of morning and has always insisted on keeping our spiritual journeys on more or less the same itinerary. For this, and much more, I am deeply grateful.

Along with the crib and the rocking chair, you had to buy another book-shelf. Now you have books about how to prepare baby food at home, books about how to get your toddler to sleep through the night, and books about teaching your child to read. You even have books about how to make your little one responsible and ethical. If all these books work, your daughter or son will be a model human being. But late at night, alone with the baby, you sometimes wonder, How am I going to raise this child's soul? What can I give her to feed her spirit that will be as nour-ishing as mother's milk? How will being a parent change me, not only emotionally and psychologically but spiritually? I asked those questions myself, but I found no book to guide me. So I decided to write this one.

Maybe you grew up in a home where religion, as one person put it, "was carried about on the hands like a holy mummy." Or perhaps your home was saturated with faith. One woman who went to mass every day throughout her childhood said, "It was like growing up with an intra-venous drip filled with spirituality attached to my arm." You may have thought a great deal about philosophical and religious problems when you were a young adult, but now suspect that as William James said, you "prematurely settled your accounts with reality."

When it rains, your child wants to run outside and feel the drops on his face. You remember the cedar pond near the summer cottage you visited as a child, and you suddenly wish you could find it again and see if it still smells so holy. You recall your own sense of wonder as you pondered life's mysteries: What happens when people die? What does the tooth fairy do with all those teeth? When people say they are "praying to God," what is really going on? You aren't sure how you will answer those questions for your child. You *are* sure you need some better answers for yourself.

When my first child was born, I had been studying religion in academic settings for twelve years. I had a rabbinical degree and the better part of a doctorate in religion. I had read many theologians, Jewish and Christian, Muslim and Buddhist. Yet as I nursed my daughter through long, gray nights the first winter of her life, I would gaze into her big expectant eyes and panic. What did I have to teach her about what really mattered? Ralph Waldo Emerson wrote, "In my dealing with my child, my Latin and Greek, my accomplishments and my money stead me nothing; but as much soul as I have avails."

I was not certain how much soul I had or if it would avail. But during those 4:00 A.M. feedings I gradually figured out one thing. All the theology I'd studied would not help me raise my children. But it might work the other way. Raising children might help me learn something about God. Theologians spend most of their time in their studies. But the best ones, I noticed, had done some fieldwork in living. I would do mine at play groups.

Within months I knew I was right. Living with small children was a crash course in all the themes I studied: love, grace, creation, revelation, forgiveness, law, suffering, power. Ten years later, it was clear that parenting was the most intensive seminar on spirituality around. I should not have been surprised. Deuteronomy says that wisdom "is not in heaven . . . neither is it across the sea. . . . It is very near to you."

The "authorities" in this book are other parents: my friends, my relatives, their friends, their relatives. I interviewed a father I met in a hotel, several former baby-sitters, and a woman one of my students encountered in a store. For a year, I sat at kitchen counters, on living room sofas, at dining room tables, on playroom floors. I visited law offices and hospitals. I even conducted one interview in the backseat of a car in the Hebrew school parking lot. Sometimes a child or two would keep us company. I asked these mothers and fathers what they did all day, all week, at special times and at ordinary times. And what they had learned about their spiritual lives from being parents.

At first, I was disappointed. One woman told me she was "too busy now to have a spiritual life"; she had put that "on hold" until the kids were older. A father suggested that I should not interview ordinary people like himself but rather ministers and rabbis because "they actually have spiritual journeys." They all agreed that being a parent had changed them profoundly, but as one put it, "I never think of mothering as having anything to do with God." Several told me that when it came to religious experience, they were "tone-deaf," or as one woman said, "It's like never having had an orgasm. I've heard about it, but I have nothing to say on the matter."

Then they went on to share the most extraordinary stories of unconditional love, of awe, of hope, of growth, of separation, of reconciliation, of sacrifice, of redemption. Emerson said, "Our faith comes in moments. . . . Yet there is a depth in those brief moments." He suggested that "there is a difference between one and another hour of life in their authority." I thought, Parenting teaches us about the faith that comes in moments, if we are willing to give those moments their authority. One father said, "I am not a religious person, but raising my children is the most religious thing I have ever done. When I think about bringing up my kids, the phrase that keeps coming to mind is 'sacred trust.' And I am not the kind of guy who uses the word *sacred* very often."

In books about sex education, the authors always stress that the least important teaching is the "big talk," the one day when you sit down and tell your child the "facts of life." Rather, education in sexuality is an ongoing process of subtle teachings and messages that together add up to a legacy for the child concerning his body, his lovemaking, his relationships. As one sex educator put it, "Sex is what you do; sexuality is who you are."

Similarly, the parents I spoke with did not report on the other "big talk"—the day the child asked, "Is there a God?," and the parent responded with a brilliant speech that you can memorize and give to your children. My informants discovered, through their journey as parents, that while theology is what you say, spirituality is who you are. Children don't listen much to what you say anyway. As for who you are, children help make you that person. Religion is passed down through the generations; spirituality is often passed upward.

This book follows the course of a single day. Compared to the cycle of the year or the life cycle, a day is very short. But so are moments. And so are children. Children slow us down when we take a walk around the block. They have to stop to collect a bird feather, to examine a candy wrapper. When writing about children, I found a single day could stretch to encompass many moments of authority. These moments may seem petty, occasioned by routine acts like changing diapers or giving a bath, made sacred only by a word or gesture or intention. Yet the little things are, in Cynthia Ozick's words, "not small but miniature," and the moments they occasion are large enough to carry us through.

When I say some moments of parenting have authority, I know from experience that some moments, even some whole summers, do not. The other day, I reluctantly ran into the nearby shopping mall on an errand. It was the first time I had been there in over six years—I hate malls. As I walked in the door, a blast of air-conditioned cold greeted me and I suddenly recalled, with embarrassment, that the summer I had an infant and a four-year-old I took the girls to that mall almost every Sunday. *Why in the world had I done that?* Why hadn't I been home reading fairy tales to them, playing imaginative games, or going on inspiring nature walks? I honestly could not remember.

As I looked around at the bright colors, the junk-food stands, the endless variety of objects to inspect, it suddenly hit me why I had gone to the mall that summer. *I was exhausted.* It was a period in which my husband was always working and my little one never slept. The mall was full of distractions—the colors for the infant, the paraphernalia for the four-year-old, the snacks for me. It required of me exactly as much as I was capable of doing at the time—walking around a cool place in a daze. There was nothing spiritually edifying for me or my children about that state of affairs or my solution for it. Sometimes we just try to get by.

When I began working on this book, however, all that would change— or so I hoped. Now I was a professional "spiritual mother"! No more secret mall life for me. I would come home each day full of excitement over something spiritual that a parent mentioned doing with her children that had never occurred to me to do with my own. One day, I spoke with a woman who reported that every night at dinner her entire family held hands, closed their eyes, and said in unison, "Let there be peace on earth and let it begin with us."

That night, as we gathered at the table I announced, "Sit down quickly and quietly, don't jump up to get the ketchup, we are now going to hold hands and pray." They squirmed but eventually took their seats. Then, in my most rabbinical voice, I announced that everyone was to find a place of peace inside themselves. I recited the words of the prayer as I had typed them on my laptop during the interview that afternoon, sat back, and waited for blessing to descend on the dining room.

Instead, all hell broke loose. The older one started singing in a raucous voice, "Let there be peace on earth . . . !" The younger one began whining because she wanted to get up and microwave her soup. Eventually, they both left the table on errands, had a collision in the kitchen, started yelling at each other, and ended in tears. Seth began to berate me for changing the rules on the kids (not to mention him) with no warning. As I sat calling for calm, the anxiety level mounted. By then I was crying too, and the vision of a peaceful dinner, much less of a world at peace, had long since been forgotten.

Later that evening, sitting in the living room reading and doing homework, we discussed what had happened. I had tried to choreograph a spiritual event. I had been bossy, not only with my family but with holiness itself. Bossiness works as poorly for a religious seeker as it does for a child on the playground. I learned that moments of faith rarely come when we expect them, and especially not when we plan them. When my younger daughter pulled off a hilarious imitation of me, we actually managed to laugh about the whole thing. While we were laughing, I knew the joke was on me in every way.

I could not prepare, serve, and feed faith to my children like homemade, nutritious baby food. But in that moment of laughter, as we moved past anger to the joy of connection, we experienced something larger than ourselves. I had read, prayed, and even preached that "God forgives our sins," but I didn't *know* that until I began forgiving my children and they began forgiving me. Forgiveness was an abundant, daily miracle, the godly in our lives. Having read Emerson, I gave the moment its full authority. I even tried to put it in the bank and live off the interest for weeks to come. That worked only for a few days. So I learned another playground rule that also applies to the spiritual life: don't be greedy.

For a year, I busied myself with my interviews, my teaching, and my family life. When I emerged, my book almost completed, I once again combed the bookstores as I had twelve years before. To my amazement, the shelves were filled with books on spirituality! There were best-sellers about angels and miracles and rites of passage. Therapists and religion scholars were marketing their wisdom.

It seemed impossible to overestimate how much my spiritually undernourished generation would spend in search of inspiration and healing. One bookstore had seven shelves of self-help books called the "Bibliotherapy" section. It seemed I was part of an as-yet-unnamed professional group—bibliopastors. Naturally, I bought every book that seemed promising.

And I learned something from each of them. There was not one that did not move me in some fashion. But I never could recognize myself in any of them. There seemed to be two kinds of books. The first kind was written by people who know just who God is and what He (as they invariably call God) wants of them. For those people, it is a simple matter to instill their faith (a known entity) in their children. In the supermarket I once found a book called *Mommy Appleseed*. I was in awe. I could envision planting my faith, like a seed, in my children, if only I knew what it was! But I am still discovering my faith as I go along. I suspect there are thousands out there, like me, with more questions than answers.

The second type of book is by people whose spirituality is only tenuously related to any historical religious tradition. In those books, I sensed a great yearning, which I share. But "generic spirituality" does not work for me; it makes me feel like I've sat down to a meal, chewed, and swallowed, but somehow I am still hungry. Trying to create a spiritual path without the "stuff" of any specific religious tradition is like, in Santayana's words, trying to communicate without speaking any language in particular. As a practitioner of an "Old Age" tradition, I am grateful for the language I have inherited. As a progressive, I believe we are making it up as we go along. But we do not have to make it up out of whole cloth.

This, then, is a book for parents who are on a quest and whose goal is not necessarily captured by the word *God* or *Goddess* or by New Age religious images. Rather, it is a search for what Paul Tillich called the "meaning within meaninglessness . . . certitude within doubt . . . the God above God, the power of being, which works through those who have no name for it, not even the name God."

Writing this book was a part of my own spiritual quest. Since I had spent so many years trying to balance my time between child rearing and religion, always feeling I was slighting one or the other, my goal was a sense of wholeness. After years of feeling torn into fragments, I was stitching my life into one piece again.

Sometimes it worked. At moments, I would have a glimpse of wholeness so profound that it seemed to unite all the parts—the funny, the awesome, the terrible, the banal. On a really good day, it even included the exhaustion of my mall-walking summer. Parents of young children in particular, live—as Emerson said—"in succession, in division, in parts, in particles." But God is where it all comes together.

This book is about how parents discover in the ordinary and extraordinary moments of their lives the reality of the unseen, the power beyond words, the place where it all comes together. And how they learn to "speak" about that reality through a language beyond language: through rituals and customs and deeds, through metaphors and stories and prayers.

An early reader of this manuscript, my friend Anna, questioned my assumption that a book about parents' spirituality should also be a book about religious practices. She agreed that parenting was a spiritual adventure, but Anna was not convinced that religion—with its communities, creeds, and practices—should be mentioned so much.

She remembers the first night she brought her baby daughter home from the hospital. "I walked around the house for hours and hours, just sensing her presence. I kept thinking, This is like being in a temple! I am dwelling in sacred precincts! It was not that my daughter was God but just that the divine was somehow in our midst.

"But I hate organized religion!" she said. "In my experience, it is religious institutions with their rules and rituals that choke spiritual experience. What I experienced that night with my baby had nothing to do with religion. I think you should stick to spirituality and keep religion out of it."

I told Anna what I believe: that in the beginning, religions were nothing more than an attempt to capture the energy she experienced that night. What she felt that night was precisely the impulse behind all those huge edifices, complicated liturgies, extensive hierarchies. Behind it all was just this simple experience. Our ancestors knew that there was more to the world than they could see or understand. When they felt themselves in the presence of the holy, they experienced a great mix of emotions: both attraction and fear, awe and dread. They created forms to domesticate the Otherness, to keep their own feelings safe and accessible. Often the forms took over and the experience got lost; religions sometimes go off track. But other times the forms really do serve as sturdy vessels.

It is my job as a religious professional to help people deepen events into sacred occasions, and I know from experience that the structures of religion can often do that. But I also understand that religion can suppress spirituality as well as nurture it. I can relate to people who call themselves "liturgically challenged." (Despite my years of rabbinical study, I still sometimes keep my finger in the prayer book at the place where the service is going to end so I can periodically count the remaining pages.) Nevertheless, I believe wholeheartedly in the power of rituals and traditions—those we inherit, those we discover, and those we create. They can help us to see the wonder in the midst of the wet diapers, whining, worry, weariness, and work.

I first realized the value of religious language one fall afternoon during my freshman year at college. I came back to my dorm room to discover my roommate, a thoroughly secular former Protestant, lighting a candle. She explained to me that she had been wandering around the campus all day in a deep depression, not knowing why. Finally, she remembered that it was October 23, the anniversary of her father's death. He had been dead for six years. Every fall, the same thing would occur. On a conscious level, she would forget the date he died. Then one day she would find herself emotionally under the weather, only to discover it was the very date she had forgotten.

This time she had decided, although she was not at all sure why, to light a candle. I did not know very much about Judaism at that time, but I did know that Jews commemorate the death of a close relative by lighting a special candle on the anniversary of their death. I found it amazing that this woman had gone to the trouble of inventing a religion for herself. I decided the least I could do was find out more about the one I had happened to inherit.

I began to take courses in Judaism. I did not like everything I discovered. But as you will see, the language of Judaism—with more than a few emendations—has proved serviceable to me. More than that, I have grown to love it. Lighting candles, or telling my daughters a Jewish folktale, or wrapping myself in a prayer shawl made for me by a friend from an Amish quilt—these acts connect me with the intuitions I have about life's depth and purpose. My goal is not to convince you to speak my language. Rather, it is to encourage you to speak *some* language, to urge you to cobble together out of your past and your present a world of images and stories and gestures and acts—what Mary Catherine Bateson called "a great rich ... bouillabaisse of human imagination and wonder"—that allows you to enliven your own journey.

Finding a path through which to express and create spiritual intuitions is an ongoing job. Once, my daughter was asked what her father did for a living. When she replied that he was a lawyer, the question came back, "Does he practice?" to which she proudly responded, "He doesn't *need* to practice. He already *knows*." Had the question been about her mother,

"Does she practice Judaism?" the answer would have had to be, "Yes. And, boy, does she need practice!" This is not a case of false humility. These are complicated times; we all need to "practice" our path until we get it right for us.

Like everything else I have done since becoming a parent, writing this book was not simple. I began work on January 4, 1994, the first day of an unpaid leave of absence from my job. Nature, with its usual poor sense of humor, contrived to ensure that my book would not be too detached from reality. My children, along with several friends, were at home with me because of an "ice emergency." A few days later, my younger daughter had an ear infection. The next day the schools were closed due to snow. Around the third week, the older child was out sick. Then it snowed again.

During the preceding fall I had carefully scheduled interviews with parents to take place at this time; now they all had to be rescheduled. And then rescheduled again. One evening, about a month after I had begun, I was typing up an interview on my brand-new laptop computer, which was plugged in to recharge. My daughter ran into my study and tripped on the electrical cord, breaking the computer and injuring her foot. Our driveway was still covered with ice.

At that moment, I knew God was trying to tell me something. I was attempting too much. *This book was not meant to be.* I recalled the Yiddish proverb, "If you want to give God a good laugh, tell God your plans." It seemed as if God was definitely laughing at this particular plan, and I would do well to honor the signs.

But having been raised on the story of Abraham *challenging* God's plans for Sodom and Gomorrah, I began to bargain. "If I can find just three days in a row to write . . . How about two days? . . . What if I found ten minutes?" There is another Yiddish proverb that says, "If God lived on earth, people would break all God's windows." So we dug out the driveway, I got the computer fixed, and I proceeded to write the book anyway.

I hope that reading this book helps you to think about your issues as a parent in a different way, to see moments in your own life as opportunities to experience the reality of God. For me, it has been a wonderful process. Retelling the stories of parents has left me in awe of the courage people bring to life's struggles. Some of the stories are about faith, which is as contagious as chicken pox among toddlers. Some are about doubts, and it is always good to know others have them too.

All of them are about mothers and fathers like you, like me, on the longest and most challenging journey of our lives. Once embarked, we cannot turn back, decide some other spiritual discipline might be more fulfilling, give back the baby, and enroll in a yoga class. For better or worse, this is our path for many years to come. May the parents in this book be good companions for you on your voyage, may they encourage you to honor your own adventure, and in the words of the Irish blessing, "May the road rise up to meet you."

Our Share of Night,
Our Share of Morning

PART I

Morning

Chapter 1

FOUR A.M.

Power and Powerlessness

*"I was God for this child, and I still
couldn't get her to sleep when I wanted."*

When I asked Chuck, a retired law professor and the father of three grown children, how he remembers the first few months of his children's lives, he waved his hand toward the porch. "Did you notice that rocking chair as you came in?" he asked me. "That's the chair in which I rocked all my children in the middle of the night. We have redecorated and moved often in the last forty years, but we would never part with that rocking chair."

With or without a rocking chair (and testimony suggests that "with" is preferable), nursing is one of the most powerful, lasting memories of early parenting. In Britain, the word *nursing* is not specifically reserved for the act of providing milk via the breast. Rather, it encompasses the acts of holding, comforting, and feeding a baby. I use the word that way, because the nursing experiences I heard about were not reserved for mothers who lactate. I spoke to fathers, to mothers who adopted children, to parents who chose to bottle-feed. All of them talked about nursing, and what they remember especially is the 4:00 A.M. feeding.

When I was in the hospital after my first daughter was born, I loved the feeding time in the dark between midnight and dawn. It seemed like the whole city was sound asleep except the mothers and babies on the fifth floor of Pennsylvania Hospital. Only hours ago, many of these tiny creatures were still in the womb. Now they were snuggling up to the freshly engorged breasts of their mothers. These newly-in-love couples finding each other in the midst of a silent, dark world were incredible. Samantha said about her nights with her baby, "It was the closest I have ever come to experiencing sacred time."

In the quiet night, a mother links eyes with a tiny soul who needs her ministrations literally to survive another few hours. A father gazes at a creature he helped to create whom he now must sustain. Parents feel enormous and small, important and vulnerable. They confront the essential paradox of parenting.

The paradox is as trivial as it is profound. Chuck remembered how the baby would fall asleep on his shoulder as he rocked him. Then the internal debate would begin. "It seems like it was yesterday," Chuck laughed. "Can I make a transfer to the crib now, or will that wake him up? But if I wait longer, will I fall asleep in this rocking chair and then drop him? I gave this child life, but I cannot make him stay asleep for thirty seconds as I lay him back in the crib."

We smile at the image of a successful law professor debating with himself on the subject of putting his baby to bed. But the issues grow more serious.

"Years later," Chuck continued, "I would lie awake at night while my son slept, obsessing over much more momentous decisions concerning the life choices we made for him or with him, and I felt exactly the same way. This kid was counting on me. I had power over his life. I always wanted to make the perfect choice, the perfect play. But there were always so many wild cards."

Parents begin to learn the limits of their power the day they first decide to have a baby or, alternatively, discover that one has been conceived despite other plans. Either way, control is not what it used to be. Liz, an older mother for whom deciding to get pregnant was a difficult choice, had trouble realizing the goal. "I was so surprised not to be able to make my body do what I wanted. By the end, it was high tech and letting go. A roller coaster. It had been years since I had even considered prayer as an activity in which I indulged. But sometimes, I found myself wishing so hard that I would conceive that it occurred to me that I was praying, whatever that meant. I remembered something a minister had said when I was a child—that when you can't do anything else to alter a situation, you can always still pray. So that is what I did."

Janet, a high-powered lawyer, told me, "My first pregnancy looked like it might end in a miscarriage. I had a huge trial coming up, and I did not want to miss it. If the miscarriage happened soon, I would be fine in time for the trial. I went to the doctor and asked him to give me a date by which it would surely be over. He looked blank. It suddenly dawned on me that he had no idea if and when I would miscarry. I ended up bleeding for months. The trial went on without me. It was during one of the many ultrasound tests when the technician kept saying, 'Oh, no!' and then 'Never mind,' that I knew the stakes were higher than they had ever been, and I was out of my league. In the end, I delivered a healthy baby, but before I even met this child, I had begun learning about my limits. That day at the doctor's office I had been handed an ultimatum in bold print: abandon control, you who enter here."

During the early months of a child's life, parents seem to fall into three main groups. For the first group, the predominant emotion is joy. For those fortunate parents, the early months of witnessing the growth of the baby's body and of their own love while breast or bottle do their work are mostly magical. "It was like being pried open with a can opener," Vivian said. "I was just leaking everywhere, overflowing. My breasts, my vagina, my heart."

Malcolm told me, "I loved getting up in the middle of the night to provide transportation for the baby to my wife's bedside. It gave me a role. I felt really needed, terrifically important. I was part of something so significant! Despite losing all that sleep, I felt grounded, whole, happy."

Pearl was also ecstatic. "I was in the Bahamas on vacation and the minute I conceived, I just knew it," she recalled. "I felt it was something greater than anything I could have just willed or made happen. As I came through customs back in the States they asked me, 'Do you have anything to declare?' and I shouted out, 'Yes, I do! A baby!' From the moment of birth, I was impressed by how much I loved him. Absolutely filled up. How could I have brought this incredible being into the world? All of a sudden, I had a clarity of purpose. I guess some people go to war to feel this. I now had a sense of my place in time and space."

For the second group, the first months of parenthood are primarily a trial. Rachel described her situation. "I was a career woman, thirty-nine years old, used to knowing what was what. Suddenly, I was isolated, overwhelmed, stuck with an impossible job assignment. I lay on the bed between nursings and tried to figure out why I had ever gotten into this mess. I started teaching myself Russian. It was something I could master, unlike the baby, and that was a great comfort."

Hank felt as though a romance was going on in which he was the odd man out. It had nothing to do with breast feeding, because he and his wife were sharing bottle feeding. It just *was*. "In the early months, I was miserable."

Lori reported, "Parenting evoked nothing spiritual in me. I felt like my self was being devoured. If anything, I would say my spiritual life began as a search for a place *away* from the parenting, for an oasis where I could find myself."

The third group is the rest of the parent population. They check: *all of the above*. For most parents, ambivalence and confusion characterize the early days of parenthood. Parents feel both ecstatic and exhausted, filled up and empty, powerful and vulnerable, thrilled and scared to death. Said one of the ambivalent many, "It was like being on a six-month honeymoon with someone who couldn't talk. It was intimate but unsettling."

Parents are unsettled by their power—and their powerlessness. On the one hand, children provide parents with a sense of potency. Sarah recalled, "There is an old story in our family about my great-aunt who weighed ninety pounds. One day a big chest of drawers fell on her small child. The tiny woman lifted the piece of furniture off the child by herself! What I got from that story was that parents have more power than they imagine. It turned out to be true. The third hour I was trying to get my infant back to sleep (a parent's version of a religious vigil!) I knew that I was too tired to go on. But I also knew that I would keep going anyway. I would think back to when I was pushing her out of me a few weeks before. I knew I could not go on, but I did. It expanded my sense of what I can do. I have more resources than I thought!"

Joan added, "To have another human being need me so much was transformative. I found out how much I could give. I loved this being so much, and it was just so incredible that she loved me back. She was so perfect and she loved *me!* For that little child being brought toward me, I was the Goddess. I held within me all she needed to sustain her life. I had never felt so full of primordial power."

Carl reminisced fondly about his short stint as the all-knowing deity. "Those early years were my one and only chance to feel what it is like to be God. When my child was in nursery school, the teacher would write parents a note on the door of the classroom each day describing what the class had done during the morning. Driving home from school, I would ask my daughter questions like 'How did you like "The Farmer in the Dell"?' Never once did she question how I was so well informed about things that had gone on in my absence. I finally realized that to her it seemed entirely appropriate that I simply knew *everything!*"

But being the one in charge is also frightening. Dora recalled her first parenting crisis: "Our daughter got a very high fever when she was three months old and needed to be taken to the hospital. I'll never forget standing there in the emergency room with my husband after the doctor had examined her. The doctor turned around and said, 'Who is responsible for this child?' We both turned around, looking behind us. Then we realized with a start, 'Oh, my God, he's talking about *us!*'"

Many parents feel humbled by the task, not quite sure if they are ready. Zoe joked, "All I can remember from the early days was the line from *Gone with the Wind* when the terrified slave Prissy shrieks, 'Me? I don't know nothing about no babies, Miz Scarlett!'"

George, a six-foot-tall gym teacher, said, "At work I got sixty strapping adolescents to jump when I blew a whistle. Then I came home and I couldn't get a twelve-pound infant to stop crying." Parents of older children continue to marvel at that paradox. Said Morris, "I can organize a convention for twelve hundred people for my organization, but when I found out I had to direct a birthday party for twelve ten-year-old girls, I was running scared. Whenever I think I am doing well as a human being, I spend a full day with my daughter and my humility is restored."

A father I met learned about limits from his child. Bert described himself as a "love junkie." "It never occurred to me that love couldn't conquer everything," he recalled. After having three healthy children of their own, Bert and his wife decided to adopt Neil, a four-year-old with serious emotional problems from his years of inadequate foster care. Despite tremendous love from the entire family, Neil's problems only worsened. "We all went to therapy and we all benefited, except him. He kept getting more difficult to control. We saw over twenty specialists. We didn't want to believe we could not fix him. He was kicked out of one school after another. Life grew darker and darker. Finally, we met a psychologist at a cocktail party who had heard our story. He said, 'Neil needs to leave your home. I will help you arrange it.' I knew we were out of our depth.

"Parenting brought me to a place of emptiness and failure," said Bert. "But ultimately, from the cauldron of this experience came learning and growth. An old religious aunt of mine said that our experience with Neil was so profound she just knew it must have meaning. I actually understood what she was trying to say. I now believe there is meaning in everything, but I no longer believe love conquers all."

Mary, too, found in parenting the wisdom to know and to accept what she could not control. In her early thirties, Mary gave birth to a Down syndrome child. After a month of grieving, she went into overdrive, signing her son up for every program and intervention available in three counties. She took him to speech therapy, occupational therapy, physical therapy. "I kept thinking to myself, I brought this child into the world, I am the one responsible for making things right for him." One day, when Jonny was six months old, Mary was with him in the swimming pool at a special class for children with mental handicaps. A mother walked in with a fourteen-year-old girl, recently disabled by a head trauma. "I said to myself, 'After all these classes, Jonny could get hit on the head! Joe—my other child—could get hit on the head!'"

It was a turning point, Mary recalled. "I didn't stop trying to make things better for Jonny, but I did give up the frantic pace. I knew I couldn't manage everything. So I decided I would do the best I could and let the rest go. For the first time in my life, I felt at peace. Having Jonny taught me that no matter what I did, it might never be enough. It takes so much energy just to do what is needed, I have none left for worrying or trying to control what I can't control."

When I was pregnant, I thought a lot about raising my children. I had developed a system for dealing with life that had worked well for me thus far. Before approaching something new, I read books about it, I took courses, I worked hard, and eventually I mastered it. All of a sudden, I had wandered into a territory in which effort and results had a more tenuous connection.

One of my favorite writers is the influential monk and spiritual genius Thomas Merton. Let's suppose I wanted my child to be the Jewish Thomas Merton. How would I arrange for that result? I looked at Merton's biography. It turns out that while pregnant with Thomas, Merton's mother read compulsively in the literature of child rearing. So would I! It also turns out that Thomas's mother died when he was four. What made him who he was? The skilled parenting of his first years or the loss of his mother when he was still a preschooler?

Whenever I think about the early days of parenting, I see myself stand-ing on the edge of a boat with my six-year-old daughter. Seth and I had taken the girls on a day cruise to go snorkeling in the ocean. As soon as the boat stopped, Seth and my older daughter, holding hands, jumped out. Then the rest of the passengers, one or two at a time, leaped into the water. Finally, I realized that the only people left on the boat were me, my daughter, and the boat captain, and he was not planning to snorkel. We stood on the edge where people had jumped. I kept fiddling with my fins and mask. My daughter tugged on my arm, "Let's go!"

Although we were both good swimmers, I suddenly realized: *I cannot jump in.* My child was holding my hand, looking into my eyes with com-plete trust and eager expectation. But the water was very deep; we could not stand. How could I go in water over my head with my child? I was to-tally paralyzed.

As we stood there, my anxiety began to creep through my hand to my daughter. "Maybe we should stay on the boat," she suggested tentatively. Then I knew: like it or not, I *had* to jump in. Over my head. My child was relying on me. I had the power to communicate my fears to my child, to make her afraid of the water. I also had the power to transcend my own fears and teach her courage. What I did not have was the power to guar-antee the world would be safe. I had to trust the water would hold us up. Without waiting another second, we jumped.

It was the same during those first weeks of parenthood. The only dif-ference was that on the snorkeling boat I could have chosen not to jump. In life, once my daughter was born, I *had* to jump, taking my child with me—into my life as a parent, into her life as a person. I had to believe the water would hold us up.

As new parents, we find ourselves jumping in over our heads, suddenly granted lifetime tenure in a job for which we have no degree, perhaps have never even taken a course. We have the power to make profound choices for someone else, choices that involve basic values and beliefs. Some of those choices are daunting.

Susan, a women's health expert, was director of a large prenatal pro-gram. Not surprisingly, she had researched and prepared meticulously for every aspect of her first child's early life: pregnancy, delivery, breast feed-ing, vaccinations. All went according to plan until something caught her off guard. During that first week at home with her son, she found herself struggling each night with an unanswered question: the religious identity of her child.

Jewish law requires a male to be ritually circumcised on the eighth day of his life. While neither Susan nor her husband had ever denied their identity as Jews, neither had they ever made much of it. All of a sudden they were confronted by a question that was in no way theoretical. The circumcision on the eighth day would either happen—or not. Nothing had prepared them for how difficult this issue would be to resolve.

As part of her work, Susan had been reading a great deal about circumcision. At that time, the women's health community was questioning its appropriateness and safety as a medical procedure. As a professional, Susan opposed circumcision. But now that they were parents, both Susan and her husband were beginning to value their Jewishness in a way they hadn't before. All things were not rational.

Between feedings, Susan and her husband discussed the pros and cons. By the eighth day, they had made a decision. They would bring their son "into the covenant" in the three-thousand-year-old manner. They were not prepared to "break the circle." They invited only their parents and siblings, their two midwives, and the ritual expert to perform the circumcision. The ceremony was held in their bedroom, with morning sun streaming in. "It was loving and intimate," Susan recalled. "It brought the birth experience, which had been so immediate and personal, into the context of our families and our history.

"We had done it! We had negotiated the first encounter between our child and the world around him. It felt great! We had made an important decision on his behalf. And having made it, we lifted the whole experience of giving birth from the plane of the physical and mundane. When the ritual was over, I turned to my sister and said, 'Now I am not only a descendant, I am an ancestor!' Those are lofty words, but that is how I felt."

Hannah, telling me about her son's baptism, said, "It was this immense relief. Until that day, I felt like I was the only one in charge of the life of this innocent, totally vulnerable baby. Now I had introduced him to God and I had a partner in my work. The priest gave us a wonderful image that day to hold on to. In *2001: A Space Odyssey*, there is a scene where the astronauts are lost in space. Two of them end up outside the spaceship. They are trying desperately to get back in. But even if they do, they'll still be lost! There's a difference, however, in being lost outside the spaceship or inside. Our religious traditions are our spaceships as we hurtle through the unknown."

The tension between power and powerlessness makes some parents want to feel part of something larger than themselves. One mother told me that when she first read the Bible as an adult with two young children, she couldn't get over how the characters sounded like the roster of her daughter's yuppie preschool—Sarah, Rebecca, Joshua. Of course, she realized it was the nursery school parents who were borrowing from the Bible, not the other way around! It occurred to her that in naming children, this very secular, postmodern generation was expressing its yearning for tradition. The sociologist Peter Berger speaks of religion as a "sacred canopy" under which the believer lives her life. Parents often find themselves reweaving their canopies, sometimes borrowing threads from afar, in order to create for their children—and themselves—a place to take shelter.

That is not all. The heightened sense of vulnerability pushes some parents to think more about the Power in the universe that is not themselves. In the major religious paths of the West—Judaism, Christianity, and Islam—God has often been imagined, metaphorically, as a parent. When people become parents, that metaphor often leaps off the page for the first time. One mother recalled, "Those first few nights, I hired a nurse so that I could get some sleep. I put three closed doors between myself and the baby. In the middle of the night, I would wake instantly when she cried. I thought about the prayer—'Lord, hear our cry!' Before, I didn't believe that God *hears* cries. But God is supposed to be our parent, and parents, I discovered, have incredibly good ears."

As Anna put it, "I was totally unprepared for the feeling of total love for this child. I finally realized that if God were my parent, this is how God must feel about each and every one of us. It makes more sense to me now."

Perhaps, as we hold and rock the fragile little ones, we too need to be held and rocked. Rocked by the Parent who, unlike us, is truly powerful. Gazing into the eyes of a child, we find the idea more plausible: that Power might be addressed as "Thou."

Not all of us can relate to a God who is called upon as "You." For many, that is an enormous leap. Nevertheless, we may still sense a Power beyond ourselves, in the world. Though we may not choose to imagine that Power as a mother or father, we may know it to be a real force in our lives.

Mara said, "With my child I experienced the strongest, most unambiguous, pure love. If that's what God is all about, then I certainly knew something of God that I had never known before."

Chuck, finishing the interview on the porch while ensconced in his old rocker, mused about those long-ago 4:00 A.M. feedings. "I could not believe it," said Chuck. "We would link eyes and it could last a half hour or more. I had always suspected that on some deep level, I was fundamentally alone in this world. But now I knew I was wrong. Being together with my child was the realest thing I had ever known. Something I had read years before by Martin Buber began to make sense. God was here in the space between our linked eyes, in the relationship, the encounter."

When recalling those early days of parenting, some mothers and fathers mainly remember the fear, others the elation. Some parents already possess a sturdy cocoon of tradition in which to raise their children. Others have to build one painstakingly, over many years. Some chat with God throughout the day; others catch only glimpses of "something more"—and that only at 4:00 A.M.

But most are filled with wonder and wondering. Wonder at the miracle of gallons of milk alchemized into yet another pound of baby. Wonder at the linked eyes (and we thought we had known something about love!). And wondering. Wondering if we have what it takes to do this job, if we can fulfill the trust. Wondering, too, after a long 4:00 A.M. feeding, how in the world we will greet the day again in just three hours.

Chapter 2

DAWN

Birth

*"When the world was first created,
it probably looked just like this morning."*

When I told people I was writing a book about the spiritual experiences of parents, many assumed that I meant the experience of giving birth. It seemed clear to them that participating in the arrival on earth of a new human being would be a "religious high." The drudgery of the next eighteen years has a less obvious connection to holiness. This chapter is about both—the extraordinary, unique experience of birth and the ordinary, quotidian experience of waking up early each morning with children. Both evoke the mystery that religious people call "creation."

For many years, on Friday mornings I went with my child to "play group." (In the interest of honesty, we should have called it "talk group" since the adults' agenda was clearly central.) One winter, we moms spent weeks on a single topic: How did other women combine children and jobs more efficiently than we? *What did they know that we did not?*

One week, Joan arrived at play group full of excitement. She had met a professional woman with three children who was publishing articles at the same rate as when she was childless. What was more, she had told Joan her secret. "All you have to do," Joan explained to a hushed and attentive audience, "is set your alarm to wake up two hours before the earliest rising child."

We were dumbfounded. It was brilliant! Why hadn't any of us thought of that? We were so desperate (and sleep deprived) that we actually believed it would work.

That night I went home and made a list of what I would do with the extra two hours. First, I would say morning blessings—something I had not done alone in years. Then, I would write in my journal. Next, I would take an aerobic walk. Finally, I would work at my computer until my daughter awoke. That night, I set the alarm, full of anticipation.

The next morning, the alarm rang. I turned it off—and promptly went back to sleep. Two hours later, my four-year-old daughter climbed into bed and woke me up, a practice she gave up just in time to turn it over to her younger sister, who has continued it to this day.

At the next play group, we checked in. The method had not worked for anyone. Then someone asked Joan who this woman was. When she told us, Susan said, "I know her! She's not even a nice person!"

Anne was exultant. "Of course not! How could she be nice? She's probably too tired!"

"Besides," Andrea pointed out, "She might get sick from so little sleep."

We all agreed that waking up too early was unhealthy at best, immoral at worst, and undeniably undoable—at least by us. We all agreed we would not wake up a minute before we had to. But once awake (admittedly, earlier than we would like), we would try to treat it as a spiritual opportunity.

What is spiritual about being up when you wish you were still asleep? For one thing, the world has been created once again. Cindy told me she had never fully grasped how beautiful morning was until her child, who had picked up some Bible stories somewhere, announced, "Look, Mom. Do you see the sky? When God created the world, it probably looked just like this morning!" This child had not heard the old Protestant hymn that begins, "Morning has broken, like the first morning." But she understood it.

Andy wanted his daughter Lena to believe the world was created, just so she could sense the mystery of it all. But he didn't believe the Bible creation story any more than he believed any other myth about the world's origins. So he bought his daughter a beautifully illustrated book filled with creation stories from all over the world. Andy's goal was not that his daughter learn how the world came to be. Clearly, on that issue opinions differ. But he wanted her to feel in her bones that it was worth pondering that there is *something* rather than nothing.

Some parents find morning a good place to begin a prayer life. Morning is such a rushed and harried time, so often lacking in moments of quiet and sanctity, that it cries out for something to elevate it, to introduce thoughts beyond "Why are there never two matching socks?" (My friend Debbie solved this problem by asking her children to safety-pin their socks together before they throw them in the laundry basket. Each time she lifts a pinned pair of socks from the basket she thinks, My children are telling me that they care, that they know these socks will go from their hands to mine and back to them.)

Harry said, "When my baby was little, if she didn't wake up in the middle of the night, we would wake up anyway and go in just to check her breathing!" (More than one father and mother made that confession.) He went on, "It just seemed so natural to start saying the Jewish prayer for waking up—'Thank you for restoring my breath to me.' When I woke each morning, I would put on my prayer shawl and just say that one verse; it was all I had time for. My daughter would often curl up in my lap while I said it. When my daughter was six, she started sleeping later than I did, but she'd often instruct me to wake her up so she wouldn't miss the prayer."

Sometimes, perhaps most times, morning prayers are uttered in a rote fashion, and the whole business is over in a few minutes. These times are not useless. A Hasidic master, Menachem Mendel of Kotzk, was once asked, "Why does it say (in Deuteronomy 6:6) that God's words should be *al levavecha*, 'upon your heart'? Shouldn't it say that they should be *in* your heart?"

"Of course they *should* be in your heart," the rebbe replied. "But that is not always possible. At the very least, you can put them *on* your heart. They may just sit there for a very long time. But someday, your heart will crack, and if they are already on top of your heart, they can slip right in."

Ritual creates its own feedback. We hold hands with a child as the sun rises, and we sense, in a way we never did before, that the world is being reborn before our eyes. Suddenly we are in the presence of the unutterable. Believing now in the world's rebirth, we choose to make that hand-holding part of our daily lives, perhaps adding some word of prayer, perhaps creating a miniritual. Along with our child, we find a language to express what cannot be spoken. Using that language over and over, we are confirmed in our initial hunch. The world is as pregnant with meaning as the sunrise with the day.

Marsha has a childhood memory of mornings when her immigrant grandmother slept at her house. "Grandma had her own morning ritual.

She would wake up early with me and take me for a walk all around the house and the yard. We would say, 'Good morning, tree! Good morning, sun! Good morning, mirror!' Sometimes we would spend twenty minutes saying good morning to our world."

Mary Lou grew up in a very religious Catholic home. Every morning, her mother would gather her family together for morning prayers. "Praying wasn't a big deal. It was like breathing. You never questioned it. I still remember what we said in the morning: 'Oh, Jesus, I offer you my prayers, works, and sufferings of this day.' I remember as a child thinking, 'I don't really do much work or suffering,' so I just moved my mouth for that part." I asked Mary Lou if she continued to say that prayer when she was the mother of ten and did not lack for work or suffering of her own. "By then I didn't have time! When I had ten children, I woke up every morning and said the shortest prayer I could—the one that I needed the most. 'Oh, God, please give me patience.' That was it."

Myrna suffered for two years with an undiagnosed, debilitating malady. Then, inexplicably, she got better. "I try to tell my children every day what it feels like to be reborn. I have no words for it, and I don't think I'm very successful, but every once in a while it feels like I am getting through. Once, in the morning, I told my daughter that just as she was getting up from sleep a new person, I got up from being so sick."

From the time he was twelve, James was a physics whiz and a cynical atheist. He still shuns all organized religion, but since his days as a graduate student in computer science, he has made room in his life for a dimension beyond hard science. One form this takes is his daily practice of yoga before breakfast. I asked James if he included his children in this practice. "They watch sometimes, but it is not a part of their lives, at least not yet."

"Do you do any morning ritual for them?" I asked.

He thought about it and then responded, "I do. But I never realized before that it was a ritual. To me, one of the most amazing clues that we don't really understand everything is dreams. I have always been fascinated by my dreams—not interpreting them, just acknowledging them. Where do they come from? When my daughter was old enough to understand, I started asking her every morning, 'What did you dream last night?' For the first year, she could not answer the question. I kept asking it anyway. Then, as she became more verbal, she began to share bits of dreams, often before I even asked. Two or three times a week, she shares something with me. Often, I will tell her a part of one of my dreams. Sometimes, she informs me that her dream was private, and that is fine too. It is a precious time for us."

Judaism prescribes blessings for ordinary events and blessings for extraordinary ones. The ordinary event, the daily rising of the sun, is greeted with a blessing that evokes a time when the world had just come into being: "We praise God who daily renews the works of creation." When it comes to extraordinary events, there is also a blessing, not well known among modern Jews, that mentions creation. The blessing is to be said "upon seeing lightning, comets, falling stars, vast deserts, great rivers, high mountains, experiencing a great storm or an earthquake, or seeing a strikingly clear morning after an all-night rainstorm." It reads, "We praise you God who provides us with moments reminiscent of creation."

When I first heard that blessing, shortly after the 1994 Los Angeles quake, I thought it was a wonderful way to frame what was otherwise a random, frightening, and senseless event. I was struck, however, that the authors of the blessing had not mentioned what by all counts is even more "reminiscent of creation" than an earthquake: the birth of a child. Alas, amazingly, there is no official blessing in Judaism for the moment of birth! But parents have confirmed what I already knew. Being present at the birth of a child, like witnessing the clear morning after an all-night rain, makes the whole miracle of creation more real. The ancient Polynesians also saw the connection between the arrival of a new life and the first stirrings of life itself. At the birth of each royal child, they would chant their creation myth, the Kumulipo.

There was a time when the world began. Having witnessed a birth, parents seem to find that notion a bit less implausible. "There we were in a room with three people . . . and suddenly there was one more!" said one mother. A midwife I interviewed told me, "Every time I assist a mother giving birth, I always prepare her in advance. I share with her my belief that at the instant she looks into the face of her newborn child for the first time, just for that second, she will see the face of God."

"I tell both my children," one mother said, "that God gave them a kiss the second before they were born, to send them on their journey. They like to hear that. And I believe it's true. They came out looking like they had just been kissed, at least to me." A father said, "I had read in *Spiritual Midwifery* [by Ida May Gaskin] that 'every child born is a living Buddha.'

I had no idea what that meant until I saw it with my own eyes. For a minute there, it seemed like the universe paused and shifted slightly to make room for this new being, totally pure and totally wise."

Several parents agreed with Rivka who said, "When my first child was born, I felt, just for a minute there, like this was the first child ever born. It felt like the ultimate miracle, and I was sure no one had ever seen anything like it." Just as a morning can feel like the first morning, so can the creation of a new human being feel like the beginning of all life.

Janet decided to have a child even though her partner Susan was not convinced she wanted to be a coparent. Susan was a skeptic. She wasn't sure she felt hopeful enough about the world and its possibilities to raise a child in it. She saw deciding to have children as a major act of faith, one she was not prepared to make. Yet when Susan was present at the cesarean birth of Janet's daughter, all that changed in an instant. "It was incredibly hard for Susan to watch someone she loved being sliced open," Janet said. "But she was amazed by the degree of sacrifice it entailed and by the whole miracle of birth. Susan was transported by the birth experience into committing herself as a coparent."

When I asked fathers about religion and birth, I cynically expected at least some of them to miss the point. One man fulfilled my worst stereotype. "It was a very long pushing, over three hours, and my wife was unable to talk. So the obstetrician and I had a long discussion about the Talmud." Most fathers, however, in almost equal measure to mothers, spoke about the birth experience as a time when they knew "something more was going on than I could ever understand."

One father told me about the personal imagery that summed up the birth experience for him. "There was a time in my life when I lived in a stone farmhouse in the hill country of Tuscany. The windows were just open spaces, no screens or panes, covered with heavy wooden shutters. At night, we would close the shutters. In the morning I would awaken in a room that was completely dark. I would get out of bed, walk to the window, and throw open the shutters. In one second, everything was transformed. Suddenly, the room was filled: with the sight of lush green hills, with golden light pouring in, with gentle breezes, with the smell of wildflowers, with the sound of hummingbirds. That was the way I felt in the minutes after the birth of our baby. Someone had just opened a window."

It is not gender that divides people so much as openness to the experience. Caryn knew something special was going on at the birth of her child, but she had nowhere to go with that knowledge. "I had been raised in a very strict Catholic home and had bought the whole thing, hook, line, and sinker. When I was twenty-one, I heard a priest praying for our boys in Vietnam, that they kill many of the enemy and come home safely. I literally walked out of that church and also *the* Church, forever. My first child was born when I was twenty-six. It was my first inkling that spiritual experience could exist outside of organized religion. I expected it to be a completely physical event—that is all my childbirth instructors talked about. Actually, the physical part turned out to be insignificant. There was something way beyond the physical that was going on. I didn't have words for it, then or now. I also had no context for carrying those spiritual feelings forward or developing them in any way.

"It was ironic! I had rejected Catholicism because it was so rigid. But in my new life as a secular person, I carried on the tradition of rigidity. I maintained a rigid idea of what religion had to be; therefore I knew it wasn't for me. My birth experiences were just that—experiences. I was with them while I had them, but they seemed confined to the event. I wish I had been more imaginative then."

Jeffrey calls the birth of his child "the most spiritual moment of my entire life." He went on to explain: "When we first discussed having children, it was hard for me to believe that I could be a nurturing, caring father. But I had nine months to get used to the idea, to put my hand on Jane's belly and feel the baby kicking, to attend childbirth classes with Jane and read all the books. The truth is, I thought the classes were for show. I was convinced that when it came to that awesome moment when the child was born, they would lock me in the closet."

I wondered why.

"I had been in the marines in Vietnam. I saw myself as a person who had been participating in organized murder and mayhem from the age of eighteen. I had killed a ten-year-old child at close range. I didn't think I could possibly be allowed to witness a birth. But I was wrong. I was there every minute. When we had counted the fingers and toes, the baby was laid on Jane's breast to nurse and I just cried my eyes out. It was only later that it even occurred to me to ask if it was a boy or a girl.

"As far as religion goes," Jeffrey continued, "my father had been a pro-war minister, and after Vietnam, the whole issue seemed settled for me once and for all. It was 'God and country' that had gotten me into that nightmare. I had no use for any of it. After my daughter's birth, I was open to new possibilities, including looking at religion in an entirely new way." Jeffrey's experience had restored his sense of the holy. For a long time, he had believed that the spirit of God was blotted out in him. Witnessing a birth rekindled that flame inside his own soul. And if it was in him, it could be throughout the universe as well.

When I asked parents about their birth experiences, they were eager to tell me the story, often in far more detail than I wanted to hear. One mother, when asked about her first delivery, began, "I called the doctor when my contractions were five minutes apart and he said to come right over." As I listened and typed, I slowly realized she was going to answer my question in exquisite detail. ". . . Then, I was at four centimeters, and Joe went out for coffee; that was at three o'clock . . ." I typed on. "The pushing was the hardest part. It lasted two hours . . ." She had been speaking for almost twenty minutes when, to my relief, "the head crowned at seven in the morning."

I realized that this mother was not answering an interviewer's question but rather engaging in a ritual recital of a religious narrative. Having studied many religious narratives and knowing the way in which their retelling functions for people, I understood that there was no use asking her, or most other parents, to "hurry up and get to the point." *Getting there* was the point. And I might as well not count on their memory being hazy. The woman I just quoted was describing a birth that had occurred forty-eight years before. And she had four more children! (Had I asked, I am sure she would have been happy to tell me about *their* births.) As she observed, "I cannot forget my own Scripture." These were events outside ordinary time, carved in her memory in a special way. Their power was evoked in the retelling.

Said one mother, "I kept a journal during the weeks just before and after my son's birth. I wanted to remember everything. It was like living in another dimension of time. I wrote down every detail of the hours leading up to his delivery. Now, each year on his birthday, I take out the journal and read aloud some part of it. He acts enormously embarrassed, but I think he secretly likes it. We are letting him know that we think his birth was a pretty big deal. As for me, it reconnects me to the magic. Some years I really need that!"

Some parents find, in the birth of their child, the birth of feelings that lead them to explore spirituality further. Said one mother, "My labor was a fairly ordinary one, but suddenly in the middle of it, I was hit by the idea—one that I had obviously known intellectually but avoided emotion-ally—that for millennia women have been doing this. For most of that time, for many women, giving birth might also mean dying. All of a sud-den, I was in this place that was midway between birth and death, on the edge of every boundary. I was freaked. But I also knew nothing would be matter-of-fact for me again. And it was not."

I know a woman whose skills as a liturgist and ritual specialist I partic-ularly admire. I was eager to ask her what she had created to mark the mo-ments immediately following the birth of her one, long-awaited child. She looked at me in surprise. "Ritual? Prayer? That was the one moment in my entire life that did *not* need a ritual or a prayer! I just was there, in that moment, fully, like a tree is there. There was nothing we could say or do that could possibly have enhanced the holiness of that time."

As I talked to adoptive parents, I learned that the miracle of creation is great enough to impress itself in a variety of ways. Alana believes that be-cause her daughter was adopted she is "even more amazing to me. I didn't create her, but when I think of all the love that it took to bring her into this life and then the wonder that of all the souls in the world we ended up together, it is fantastic!"

Barbara had assumed, ever since her hysterectomy at age twenty, that she simply wouldn't be a mother. When she and her husband finally de-cided to adopt, she was apprehensive. At the airport, the tiny Korean baby girl was placed in her arms and all doubts vanished. "That I could give my heart so fully to a total stranger from across the globe seemed utterly fan-tastic. The heavens opened. Right there in the middle of the terminal." About missing the chance to be a biological parent, Barbara says, "I know I'd feel differently about my child if I had borne her. But I cannot possibly believe that I'd love her more."

Families handle the rituals celebrating the adopted child's birth in dif-ferent ways. Alana sees the day of her child's actual birth as a time to think about the woman who bore her daughter. Together Alana's family lights a candle for that faraway woman, unknown to any of them, and they say a prayer for her, giving thanks for her and wishing her blessings. The party and presents are reserved for "Welcome Ellen Day," the anniversary of the day she was adopted, the day the miracle occurred when they became a family.

Barbara, on the other hand, celebrates with cake, balloons, and all the usual hoopla on the day her daughter was born. "After all," she reasons, "she came into the world just like any other kid and should have a party on her birthday just like them. Adopted kids need to know they are like other people, born of flesh and blood in that same miraculous way. The day she came to our home is an anniversary we like to mark, but in a quiet way. Our tradition is to go for a special walk in the woods."

Whether it occurred in delivery rooms or airport terminals, women and men report that "the heavens opened" when their life as parents began. And that, as they say, is the least of it. "Sure, I fell in love when I first saw each of my children," my friend Judy said. "If you want to call it a moment of revelation, go ahead. But to me it is like falling in love with my husband. The first date was only the beginning. I fall in love with Steve over and over again, as we go through our lives together. I am much more in love now than I was the night we met. It is the same with the children."

That is why the blessing says God *renews* creation daily. Each morning is an opportunity to relive those moments of birth and connection and also the moment at the beginning of time—the one we can only imagine through stories. Each morning our souls are returned to us, our world is recreated for us, we are reunited with our children. Each morning we can celebrate this.

What if it were not so?

One of my favorite stories is about the first man, Adam, on the very first day of his life. Night came, and since this was the first time Adam saw darkness, for all he knew, this was it. The black would envelop him and he would never again see the sun, see the animals he had named, see the woman who had been created as his soul mate. So he sat through the night wondering, fearing. And then, as dawn approached, the process he had watched with such sadness the night before began to reverse itself. The sky grew lighter, the birds sang again. Another day had begun. With relief and gratitude, Adam rejoiced.

Our first child was born at 1:00 A.M. on a Friday in December. At ten later that morning, my husband taught a hundred law students the last session of the semester's course. Years later, I ran into a former student of his who had been in that class. I had always assumed that not having slept in over twenty-four hours, Seth had dragged himself through the period. "I still remember him that morning," the student said. "Someone in the back row scratched his head, and the professor noticed it. I have rarely seen anyone so awake."

One of the great religious traditions of the world is devoted to the teachings of a man named Siddhartha Gautama. Once someone stopped him on the road and asked, "Are you a god?"

He denied it adamantly.

"Well, then, are you a celestial being?"

Again the answer was no.

"Perhaps you are a wizard."

Once again, he disagreed.

"Then what are you?"

The man replied, "I am awake."

The Buddha and those who followed him understood that really to be awake is no small matter.

True, with children around, we see more dawns than we might choose. On the other hand, really to see a dawn is no small matter.

Chapter 3

GETTING DRESSED

Bodies

*"Why is Grandma uncomfortable
with my clothes? It's not her body!"*

Having greeted the dawn, the parent must now face the day. Having connected your soul to your child's soul or not, as the case may be, you now
must address the question of bodies. For years before we can talk together, read together, pray together, we parents take care of our children's
bodies. We feed them, diaper them, dress them, bathe them, watch them
grow. As we engage in these processes, those of us whose spirituality had
been ethereal or intellectual begin to see things differently. They have
bodies, and (in case we had forgotten) we too have bodies. "I was a person
who lived in my head," said Norman. "Then the baby arrived." Often,
surprisingly, some of the great spiritual moments of parenting come when
we are up to our elbows in stuff.

Caring for the bodies of children is an opportunity to reflect on their
beauty, on their quality as images of the divine. The Bible forbids making
pictures or statues of God because every human being is God's image.
Caring for the image of God is a commandment. A story is told about
Rabbi Hillel and a bath. Once, his disciples asked where he was going.

"To perform a commandment," he replied.

"But where are you going?" they asked again.

"I am going to the bathhouse."

"Is taking a bath a commandment?" they challenged him.

"The king's statues set up in theaters and circuses all over the city are
scoured and washed down by officials," he replied. "How much more am

I required to scour and wash down myself since I am created in the image of God!"

Parenting may be a spiritual journey, but it is never far removed from bodily realities. During pregnancy, as a woman's shape changes to accommodate the growing fetus, she is often more aware than ever that she is a body as well as a mind and soul. Debbie remembers being pregnant and watching the family cat nurse her kittens and purr. "It got me in touch with my animal sense. I wasn't so different from the cat after all. It gave me permission to give in to that part of me."

My own first pregnancy unfolded during the summer and fall of 1982 while I was serving as a rabbi in New York City. The congregation drew its members mostly from my grandparents' generation. I approached the fall High Holidays (the Days of Awe) seven months pregnant. Several of my congregants suggested that I consider wearing a robe to lead these important services, although neither I nor my predecessors had ever been so formal. I accepted their suggestion, agreeing that the solemnity and awesomeness of those holidays would be enhanced by making my distinctive body a nonissue. Later, when I thought about it, I decided that I had made the right decision for the wrong reason. I had thought that my huge pregnant body might be an affront to the holiness of the occasion. In fact, it was simply *too* awesome.

While all women feel physically altered by the birth of a first child, some feel utterly transformed. Jane told me, "When my first child was born, I had a strange physical reaction. My face swelled up and there were hemorrhages in my eyes. The doctor said it was due to a minor blood-clotting abnormality and that for a few weeks I would look like I had been severely beaten. Every time I saw myself in the mirror during that time, it underscored that I had really gone through a big deal. It was an outward manifestation of an inward change."

When I told other new mothers this story, they understood immediately and seemed almost envious of Jane. Said Rosalie, "I looked the same in the mirror as I had before, which somehow seemed weird. I certainly didn't *feel* the same!"

Alice reported, "Right after the birth of my baby, I was very proud of my body and felt most warmly toward it. After all, look what it had accomplished for me! Sure, it was still much bigger than I was used to, and I wanted to lose the weight I had gained. But that had nothing to do with my love for my body. I would stand in the shower, watching the water bounce off my skin, off my flabby belly, and rejoice. In the shower I composed a whole series of poems that I never had time to write down. Their title was 'Ode to My Body.' "

The baby arrives, squirming and howling, very much a body. Kevin confessed that he was enthralled by his newborn's smell, as if it provided a whiff of another world. "I never told anyone, but for over a week after we got home we did not give her a bath," he admitted. "We didn't want anything about her to change."

I never understood the Christian idea of God's incarnation until I had a child. A few months after my pregnant High Holidays, Seth and I were sitting in our living room on December 24, marveling at our six-day-old first child. The doorbell rang and there was Father Gerard Sloyan, the chairman of my doctoral dissertation committee. Fearing that he was in search of some finished chapters, I hastened to inform him that I had accomplished nothing much in the last month except this small bundle in my arms. Father Sloyan assured me that he had no thought of my dissertation but had stopped in only to visit the small bundle. "It is the Lord's birthday tomorrow," Father Sloyan explained, "so I wanted to hold a baby in my arms." Having studied Christianity, I had read about incarnation, but for the first time I really "got it." In the Christian imagination, God was once a tiny body just like this!

Mothers who used their own bodies to nourish their child's bodies through breast feeding wanted to talk about it. A lot. Magda, a nurse and a single mother of one son, insisted that she was "not at all religious." Nevertheless, near the end of our interview, she told me that she did have a spiritual experience "that lasted not for minutes but for months." It was breast feeding. "I am moved most by nature and by camaraderie. Breast feeding is both. For me, feeding my child with my own body was the perfect interconnection, the linking of the physical and the emotional. It was the ideal circle in which there was no glitch. The first time I nursed I had a revelation: so this is what breasts are for!"

Gloria, a psychotherapist, told me about going to work during her breast-feeding months and listening to her clients talk. Whenever they began to speak about need or longing, she could feel her breasts fill up with milk. "My body was actually responding to what I heard. It was the most extraordinary thing my body has ever done."

Cathy went back to work while still breast feeding. While sitting at her desk across town, she would notice her breasts beginning to leak—in effect, crying out to be nursed. She'd call home to check in with the babysitter, and sure enough, the baby had just begun to cry. "I believed my baby and I were communicating across the miles. It was the most intense experience of connection I have ever had."

For some, breast feeding is a new experience of bodily connection, different from the sexual, adding another dimension to their lives. Lila remembers, "For me, the milk was a living metaphor of God's love. The more the baby needed, the more milk there was. If the baby took less, there was less. Now, how did the breasts figure that out? I could never get over it. But the more love we need from God, the more there is."

Along with feeding a child comes its inevitable complement, the child's excretion of bodily waste. Here we come to perhaps the most mundane and earthy side of the whole baby business, yet it, too, has its spiritual lessons. "My husband and I were amazed to realize how much time we spent discussing bowel movements," laughed Jeanette. "In our whole married life, we had *never* discussed bowel movements. Now we did, even at the dinner table—once, even when there were guests! It made us less pretentious. After all, this is basic human stuff, and we were not exempt."

The business of toilet training is for some parents a fascinating study in bodily autonomy. "My son was the toughest case of toilet training you will ever hear of," Melinda complained with only partially disguised pride. "He wanted no part of any of it. He refused to even sit on the toilet to give it a try. We talked and talked about it, but there was no action. Nothing. He and the toilet never made contact." Then the time came for his three-year-old checkup. "The doctor said I needed to bring a urine specimen. I explained this to my son, and he agreed to sit down on the toilet the next morning. And he did, at 6:30 in the morning. At 11:00, he was still sitting, still refusing to pee. At noon, we had to leave for the doctor, so I gave up and put a diaper on him. He just flooded that diaper! I cannot imagine how he held all that in for so long! I drove off to the doctor without the sample, certain I would be buying diapers for the rest of my life. But the very next morning, my son woke up, took off his diaper, walked over to the toilet and peed, went back to his room, and put on a pair of underpants. We never discussed the topic again. I guess he had proved to himself that it was *his* body and he was in control, so now it was OK to use the toilet."

How was all this a spiritual experience for Melinda? "I so respected his passionate journey to figure out what his body was capable of," she says. "I saw him for the first time as bone of my bone, flesh of my flesh, and yet so completely his own flesh, his own being, not prepared to part with what was his until his own good time. I found myself in awe of the process we all go through to become our own people, to claim our own space, and I was much clearer than ever how it all starts with the very bodies we inhabit. No, not inhabit, *are*. It was an occasion for wonder."

Parents often must face the reality of their child's essential separateness. I called Stuart, expecting a wonderful "body story" because I knew about Stuart's own interest in the physical. "When I was younger, I played a variety of sports, and now, I am happiest when I am hiking or rollerblading," Stuart said. "For me, exerting myself physically, being 'in my body' is the most important part of the day. It is the time when I am most alive, when I am uplifted psychologically and also spiritually. As a scholar, I devote much of my research to issues of the body."

Stuart is now the single father of a seven-year-old daughter. Naturally, he expected her to join him in his love for physical activity. But Tammy, like many children, challenges her father to give up his expectations. "It turns out Tammy doesn't like being physically active. I had so looked forward to the joy of teaching her each of the sports, of running and hiking with her. But she is simply uninterested, at least so far. Her own passions are all sedentary pursuits. When I try to cajole her into engaging in my agenda, we both end up frustrated. Only when I respect her own way of using (or not using) her body do we really do well together."

The tiny bodies of our children often seem to evoke powerful emotions. Janet said about her infant son's body, "I keep trying to figure out why I react so strongly to Jack's body. What is it about him and the way his skin is so smooth, the license I have as a mother to indulge in the sensuality of touching it, the innocence and sheer beauty of it all?"

Said another mom, "Once I was sitting with my two-year-old on the floor watching a video, and he decided he wanted to play with the control panel on the TV set. I set myself up as a barricade so that he would have to crawl over me to get to the TV. He was climbing all over me, having an absolutely fabulous time, and it occurred to me that the best jungle gym, the best toy for my son, was my own body. He was climbing up my back and I thought, We are a sculpture. Somebody looking down at the two of us would see a living, breathing sculpture of two human beings. It was a moment of awe for me—we were art."

Suzi said that the responsibility for her children's bodies ultimately led her to take better care of her own. "When my first child was born, I spent hours in the library reading about health and medicine. I did not want to trust doctors; I wanted to think everything through for myself. I felt my children's health was a precious gift with which I was entrusted. As I learned more, I started to feel that way about my own health.

"I had always taken the workings of my own body pretty much for granted. But now I began to really care for myself. At this point, I would not even dream of smoking, drinking, taking drugs, or driving fast—activities I tried out when I was childless. It is not just because I want to stay healthy to see my children grow up, though I do. And it is not just to set a good example for them, though that is important too. It is mainly because I feel, in ways I never did before, how precious my body is."

Then there is the matter of dressing our children's bodies. Not the spiritual high point of the day, you say? For a long time, it is something we simply have to do, part of the daily routine. God clothes the naked, and we clothe our children. But as our children grow older, the whole issue becomes more complex. Can they put on their own clothes? How much help do they want? Sometimes more than they need, sometimes less. Most toddlers want to dress themselves independently *and* want someone to take care of them. They often don't know which they want more. Parents want their kids to grow up and take care of themselves, yet they also want to maintain the closeness and control. And speaking of control, who decides what gets worn?

At stake here are not just shirts and pants. Do we really see our child as an autonomous body or as an extension of our own bodies? When children are small, we dress them exactly the way we want. We impose on their bodies our vision of who they are. When my younger daughter was a baby, I occasionally found myself engaged in minor warfare with her baby-sitter over what my daughter would wear. In the morning, I would dress her in a comfortable stretchy sleep suit, one of several worn hand-me-downs from a friend. When I came home, I would find my daughter turned out in a starched, lacy dress, a birth present that I had hidden in the back of one of her drawers. Barbara, the baby-sitter, would mutter something about her "needing to be changed," but I knew better. Barbara was indeed "changing" my daughter so that she could look more like an extension of Barbara than an extension of me. I didn't mind. (At least that is how I like to remember the story.) It is part of what we do with babies.

When children get older, however, they want to use their bodies to display their own identities, not ours or the baby-sitter's. One wise mother let her daughter feel her oats. "For a year or two, she would wear only purple—ever. So we went out and bought a lot of cheap purple clothing. My mother and I had had horrible battles over my clothing, and I didn't want to replicate that. I figured, it is a safe arena for her to be herself."

Other parents I spoke to agreed. "Kids don't have many choices," one of my friends said, "so I let them use clothes as an expression of themselves and their autonomy."

Sometimes, however, children's choices conflict with the parent's agenda. Valerie told me how important it was to her that her sons dress up for the Sabbath, to honor the specialness of the day. Unfortunately, the boys did not see it that way. They wanted to wear sweatpants just like they wore all week, not uncomfortable dress clothing.

Finally, Valerie came up with a compromise that respected their instincts and her concern for the holiness of the day. She took them to the store and let them pick out wild, colorful, patterned sweat suits. These suits would be worn only on the Sabbath and then laundered so that they would be clean the following week. They were comfortable but special. Valerie confessed, "The truth is, the clothes aren't really fancy so much as they are funny. But at least they are designated."

In the teen years, the battles over whose body it is recur, with issues about appropriate dress, makeup, ear piercing, tattoos, hairstyles and dyes, and the like. It is not surprising that these become important battlegrounds between parents and children as children claim their bodies as their own.

Nina understands the power of clothing. She grew up among the Old Order Amish in Lancaster County. At the age of twenty-six, Nina chose to break a central rule of her religion and to attend college, even though she knew this would result in her excommunication. The night before the church service in which she would be officially dismissed from the community, she went out to the field and talked with her bishop; they both cried. Then, on the train to Chicago, she went to the ladies' room, changed into modern clothing, and wrapping her Amish dress and hat in a small bundle, threw them out the window.

Linda, a feminist who lives in Los Angeles, faced the greatest clothing challenge that I heard about. As usual, the magnitude of the challenge was directly correlated with the magnitude of the learning it afforded. At age two, Linda's only child, Jeff, grabbed one of Linda's T-shirts and happily announced: "This is my dress!" He often would wear a long T-shirt to day care. Soon he began asking for dresses of his own. At the store, he would beg for all manner of pink, frilly, lacy clothing—especially skirts and dresses. Linda was unsure how to handle the situation. She wanted to let him play it out in his own way. He was a happy, friendly, industrious boy.

By the age of four, Jeff—still happy and well adjusted—understood that at school he needed to wear pants and not dresses. Home, however, was another matter. As soon as he got in the door, he would run to his room and change into "something pretty"—a bride's dress, a Cinderella costume, his mother's skirt. When the family went visiting, he would ask if this was the kind of place where he could wear what he wanted. If not, he would content himself with regular boys' clothes. But if it was, he would pack a huge suitcase full of his beloved outfits. Once, his mother explained that his dress habits made his grandmother uncomfortable. Genuinely puzzled, he asked, "Why do they make *her* uncomfortable? *She's* not wearing the clothes. It's not *her* body."

Jeff is now thirteen and has ceased showing any interest in girls' clothing. But Linda believes she learned a great deal from her son. "For one thing, I have been forced to confront my own prejudices and fears," she explained. "I thought I was a pretty hip, tolerant person. But Jeff made me wonder. When he was so interested in dresses, I thought this may all blow over in another year or two, or it may mean something about him. So I had to read and consider how I would feel if my son turned out to be gay. I even have had to imagine how I would feel if he were a transsexual and ultimately chose to have a sex-change operation. This pushed me to a point where I made a wonderful discovery: I loved my child deeply and totally, no matter what his sexual orientation or even gender turned out to be. I didn't love a little boy, I loved a little person.

"This led me to some new realizations about God. When feminism first began and a lot of us became skeptical of all the male God language in our tradition, I—along with many others—began to experiment with calling God "She" or "Mother" or even "Queen." But it always felt to me a little like dressing the male God up in drag. Now, I think I see this even more clearly. The names for God are just like clothing. Just like the essence of my son was not tied up with his gender, so the essence of God is beyond gender."

While we are busy diapering, toilet training, dressing, and fighting about clothing, a miracle occurs. The little body we cared for becomes bigger and bigger, more and more its own separate person. "In only twelve years," Joe said, "my daughter went from a tiny creature, smaller than the chicken we roasted for dinner, to a shapely young female, taller than any woman I ever dated. One day she seemed part of us; all of a sudden we turned around and she was a being of her own."

We had a kind of sacred shrine in our home for years, a place that evoked wonder every time I walked by it. The shrine was created around an idea in a work by Mordecai Kaplan, a great American Jewish religious thinker whose version of Judaism—Reconstructionism—is the kind I practice and teach. In one of my favorite passages, Kaplan writes, "There can hardly be a more real and more God-revealing experience in the inner life of a child than that of growth. Every child realizes how much bigger and stronger physically . . . he grows with every year. . . . It is not something he can get himself to do at will. . . . It happens to him as it does to [plants and animals]."

Because the physical growth of our children seemed as miraculous to Seth and me as it did to Kaplan, we began marking on our front hall archway each of our children's heights, along with the date, every six months or so. While the realtor who appraised our house for possible future sale disapproved of the defacing of our walls, for us, this chronicle of the children's growth definitely belonged in a privileged place in our home.

One summer, we arranged to have our house painted while we were on vacation. Alas, we returned to discover that we had forgotten to tell the painters about our shrine! It was all neatly painted over, a clean white hall that would make a realtor rejoice. Saddened by the loss of nine years of records, we resolutely picked up where we had left off, using bold markers to make permanent the mystery of bodies growing.

Chapter 4

SIBLINGS

Connection

*"My favorite part was when my brother
said he was connected to* me.*"*

At 12:30 P.M. on April 4, 1991, the playground at our local elementary school was filled with noisy, carefree children. Two minutes later, two small airplanes, one carrying a U.S. senator, crashed in midair and landed in flames on the school playground, killing all the passengers. When the chaos had abated and the schoolchildren had all been accounted for, two had died, one was seriously burned, and the rest badly shaken but physically unharmed. Five years later, people in our community still talk about that afternoon.

I asked a third-grade teacher what she remembered most vividly. "I'll never forget the reaction of the children. They were terrified, of course. We were trying so hard to get the kids back to their classrooms, but the kids had a different agenda. 'Where is my brother? Where is my sister?' Every one of them with a sibling in the school had the same concern. That morning at breakfast, two brothers may have been teasing each other mercilessly, but now their only thought in the nightmare was to make sure the other was OK."

As Marian Sandmaier, the author of a book about siblings called *Original Kin*, points out, our sibling bonds are the longest-running relationships of our lives. In most cases, we encounter our siblings before we meet our friends and partners, and we continue to know them after our grandparents and parents are gone. We compete with them, we live out roles defined by them, we measure ourselves against them. They are our earliest and longest-lasting experience of connectedness, of sharing. The bond is deep, primal.

Hugo took his sons, Steve and Ian, to a church breakfast. Before the pancakes were served, everyone was asked to say their name and whom they were connected to. That night Hugo asked six-year-old Ian what he had enjoyed most about the morning. "My favorite part," Ian said, without hesitation, "was when Steve said he was connected to *me.*"

When my younger daughter was three days old, it was time to bring her home from the hospital to meet her four-year-old sister. Waiting in the hospital lobby for Seth to get the car, I sat down on a couch with the baby in my arms, directly behind an elderly woman talking to a doctor. The woman was quizzing the doctor on how to care for her seriously ill older sister who, it became clear, was a patient in this hospital about to be released into her care. At that moment, I imagined the baby in my arms as a seventy-five-year-old, inquiring how to care for her seventy-nine-year-old sister.

That image has sustained me through many rough spots over the years. For along with the deep connection comes, as any parent will attest, fierce competition. For example, there was the night the children had head lice. We were discovering the literal meaning of the metaphors "nit-picking" and "fine-tooth comb" as we went to work trying to find and remove the tiny nits from the girls' hair. (My friend Mary, who had been through many cases with her child, had told me that the disease was never fatal—except to the sanity of the parents.) As we methodically combed and picked, we commented on how many nits we were removing from each head. Suddenly, our younger daughter began to cry. "It's not fair! My sister has more head lice than *I* do!"

Of course, all siblings experience competitiveness. Ben told me about the time he took his children on a hike in upstate New York on a trail that passed through deep forests and sparkling waterfalls. "At the trailhead, there was a stack of biodegradable shopping bags with a sign asking hikers to collect any trash they found on the trail," he recalled. "For the next hour, we walked through indescribably beautiful scenery as my boys fought over each beer can and cigarette wrapper we passed along the trail."

Janice's daughter loves true stories about herself, and the one she never tires of is the story of her birth. "I had gone into labor around midnight," Janice began. "We had parked our older sons, asleep in their pajamas, at a neighbor's and gone to the hospital. But when we got there, the labor slowed down. I even slept most of the night. In the morning, I decided to call to see how the boys were doing. As I dialed the number, a huge labor pain rocked me nearly out of the bed. I hung up the phone without saying a word, and ten minutes later, our youngest child entered the world, kicking and screaming. I cannot begin to describe the satisfaction my daughter gets out of hearing about the moment when *her* needs took center stage. Nor can I count how many times she has made me tell her that story."

How do parents feel about their children's rivalry? What does it bring up for them when their children fight? I asked this question of parent after parent. The response was unanimous: "It makes me crazy. It is the hardest thing in the world."

How do parents deal with sibling rivalry? Harvey reported that in his family sibling rivalry—or at least its expression—was always diffused by a brief sermon. He would simply say, "In this house are the people who are going to be there for you no matter what. These are your long-term allies. Don't even consider meanness." A book I read suggested that when children fight with each other, the parent should intervene and take them both for a walk to a beautiful spot where they can sit and pray together. Needless to say, these solutions require parents who are unusually centered and, in the latter case, blessed with an unusual amount of free time.

Clara shared with me a ritual she designed when her three grade school daughters were involved in daily scrapes. She told the girls that there would be a special event later that afternoon and that each of them had to find a present—something really wonderful—for each of her two sisters. The girls scurried around the house finding the presents. When the time came, the four of them sat together on the floor and Clara lit a candle in the center. Then, one at a time, each girl gave each of her sisters the gift she had selected, looking into her eyes and telling her that she loved her. When the gifts were distributed, the girls held hands and made a pact that if they ever lost the sense of love and connection they had at this moment, they would cough twice. Then their sisters would know to reach out extra hard. When the vow was made, they all lay down on the ground with their heads together in the center and blew out the candle.

Several parents reported that family meetings helped to strengthen a sense of connection among siblings. Grace, who had only been practicing the art of family meetings for a short time, was very excited about the process. "Every Saturday morning, we sit down together on the floor and we have appreciations. Everyone says something nice about each of the other family members. Then we have announcements and divide up the chores for the week. At the end, we all hold hands. I have noticed a kinder spirit permeating the rest of the week."

Sandy, a veteran parent, held family meetings each Thursday night for twenty years. Sandy had grown up in a traditional churchgoing family but had left organized religion when she married a man of a different race. Raising her children in an interracial home in the fifties and sixties was not easy. Family meetings were "sacred" time, attended by everyone and faithfully tape-recorded. The tapes accumulated in a dresser drawer and were rarely listened to; nonetheless, the taping enhanced the importance of the occasion.

"Each meeting had a chairperson, a job that rotated among the parents and children," Sandy recalled. "When a child reached the age of six, the child could take on the job of chair. Each meeting had the same format: happy, angry, sad. The chair would announce the topics one by one, and each family member would share something from the week that fit the category—what had made them happy, angry, and sad that week. When we first moved to a new neighborhood and the children were experiencing a great deal of racism, the angry and sad sections took quite a while. The children learned that when they were hurting, the best resource in the world was their family."

Another difficult aspect of sibling relationships is the way in which brothers and sisters tend to get stuck in roles. Andrea told me this story: "One sunny, icy Saturday afternoon, I rushed into the kitchen from grocery shopping, my arms filled with bundles. Before I could set them down, I saw open on the kitchen table the *Merck Medical Manual*. On the top of the page it said, 'Head Trauma.'"

"Where is she?" Andrea yelled, running into the living room to find her husband sitting on the big black recliner with a dazed and gray daughter in his arms. Their five-year-old, Wendy, had just fallen on the ice. She couldn't remember anything for more than two minutes and complained that her head hurt. The pediatrician had been paged and would call back "soon."

During the next three days, Wendy regained her orientation but continued to have headaches. After several trips to the hospital emergency room and much worry, she was diagnosed with a "mild concussion." Andrea had a list of trouble to watch for: stiff neck, vomiting, serious head pain. And watch she did. Constantly. After a week, the doctor declared the event completed.

"What am I to watch for now?" Andrea wanted to know.

"Nothing," he said. "Forget the concussion ever happened. Your daughter is herself again."

"But Wendy wasn't herself in my eyes," Andrea told me. "I was still watching for the signs, still expecting her to have headaches. She was returning to her old self, although more cautious. I even overheard her saying to a friend, 'Be careful on the ice or you'll slip and get a mild concussion.' A week or so later, a friend of ours who was a family therapist told me about two adult brothers whom she treated. One of the brothers had a concussion at age ten. Even as adults, they were still locked into their roles. One was the 'bright boy,' the other 'the concussion.' To me, my daughter was still 'the concussion,' and I began to notice how my special concern for her was affecting her relationship with her brother."

Andrea understood that Wendy now needed to say good-bye to her "sick girl" role and be welcomed back into the family as "regular Wendy," occasionally sick, usually well, always normal. That night, a Thursday, as her family sat around the dinner table, Andrea announced, "Tonight we are going to make Havdalah" (the ritual that separates Sabbath from the weekdays).

Doing a ritual at the wrong time is bound to get people's attention. "But it isn't Sabbath!" the kids protested. Andrea said she realized that, but she wanted everyone to say good-bye to sick Wendy and welcome back regular Wendy, just as the family said good-bye to Sabbath and welcomed back the weekdays. "So we did the wine and spices and candle, and everyone told a little about how they felt when Wendy was sick, and then we thanked God she was better. In that way, we separated ourselves from the experience—and freed Wendy to be herself again."

Andrea's story made me think about the part religion can play in supporting or undermining family dynamics. Sibling rivalry and roles were an issue in my family of origin and now again in the family in which I am the mother. Since I peddle the healing power of religion, I wanted Judaism to speak to me and to my children on this issue. I kept my ears and heart open, and eventually I was rewarded.

When my older daughter turned twelve, we began to discuss her Bat Mitzvah, the Sabbath near her thirteenth birthday when she would publicly read from the Torah scroll for the first time. After deciding on a Bat Mitzvah date, we consulted the special calendar to discover what portion of the Torah she would be required to study and chant. Her portion included the story of Rachel and Leah. Since she is a girl with one sister, I was confirmed in my hunch that this kind of thing is never entirely accidental.

I had, of course, read the story. I knew that Rachel and Leah were classic sister rivals, frozen into opposing roles and full of envy for each other. I knew their father, Laban, would have benefited from the services of a good family therapist. (And where was their mother, anyway?) Rachel was beautiful, Leah fertile. Jacob, the third patriarch, fell in love with Rachel but was tricked into marrying her older sister Leah as well. Rachel had Jacob's love but not his children. Leah had Jacob's children but not his love. They both wanted what the other had. By the end, somehow or other, Rachel had two children as well. Then she died. As far as I could remember, the story was fairly depressing.

As my daughter went to work, I began to study the portion again myself. When I finally read the whole story carefully with commentaries, I discovered to my surprise that there was one detail I had always skipped over. Leah possessed some mandrakes, a plant believed to promote fertility—the very thing her sister wanted. Rachel purchased them from her sister in exchange for a promise that she would instruct Jacob to spend the night with Leah. Each gave up the thing that the other most desired, and each achieved what she most wanted. It was only when the sisters worked together that Rachel finally conceived.

For the rest of her life, my daughter will remember that she became an adult member of the Jewish people as she chanted the story of two sisters who were "set up" to be rivals. Yet they transcended their roles to become allies. Even as they were both victimized, they found a small way to reach out to each other.

The alliance with our siblings can nurture and sustain us throughout life. One of my friends, Phil, learned this in a most dramatic way. When his sister was dying of leukemia, doctors informed the family that her only hope was a bone-marrow transplant from the matching marrow of a sibling. On three different occasions, Phil traveled long distances, missed weeks of work, and compromised his own health to give the very marrow of his bones to his sibling.

Marian Sandmaier, the author of *Original Kin*, read this book in manuscript and encouraged me to listen for "the dog that wasn't barking." At first, I did not know what she meant.

"You have stories about competitive siblings and stories about connected siblings. You quote parents whose love expands to include all their children equally and—here's where the silence is. You don't explore the dilemma of parents who really do favor one of their children over another."

"That's because no one I interviewed shared with me a story along those lines," I responded.

"Of course they didn't. A parent's struggle with his own favoritism is not something he will usually choose to bring up," Marian explained. "Parents believe they should love all their children equally—even identically—and they are often ashamed to admit otherwise. But if you ask almost any parent with more than one child, you will find out the truth."

So I headed for my local bookstore, ordered a cappuccino, and waited till a parent I knew came through the door. I put him on the spot and quickly learned that Marian was right. He told me, "Please don't use my name. I hate this about myself. But one of my sons, Gene, is the child I always wanted: athletic and fun-loving. The other one is more artistic and intellectual. I know, in theory, that I should spend equal amounts of time with both of them. And I guess I do love them both equally, but I cannot help it. If given a choice, I would always rather be with Gene."

After this father left, an old friend joined me at the table, and I posed the question of parental favoritism again. It turned out that she, too, agonized over her different reactions to her two children. "It is not just a question of one sharing my interests and one being different from me. Actually, the girls are quite similar on the surface. It is a much more visceral thing. When my older daughter was a baby, she would cry as if to say, 'Please, come in here, it would be nice to get fed.' My younger child's cry was different. It said loud and clear, 'Get in this room right this minute or else.' The strange part is, it is the younger daughter that I feel closer to. This isn't something I can quantify or describe. There is just this tug inside me that is stronger toward her."

Indeed, once I began to ask the question, it seemed that nearly everyone struggled with favoritism. Some parents felt especially drawn to their oldest child, some to their youngest, some to the child who was most like themselves, some to the one who was most different. One of my friends, after seeing the movie *Sophie's Choice*, began to have a recurring nightmare. In the movie, the heroine is forced to choose which of her children she will hand over to the Nazis. In my friend's dream, she is presented with Sophie's choice. Part of the terror of the dream, my friend explained, was realizing that she actually *did* know which child she would choose. "Over the years, the dream lost some of its horror," she said. "To my surprise, as the years passed, the child I would choose changed, and then changed again. Perhaps knowing this would help young parents be less concerned about their favoritism."

Linda's concern was not so much favoritism as limited resources. She worried about having enough energy to meet everyone's needs. "My kids compete a lot over the scarcity of my attention. The truth is, my love for each of them is limitless, but being only one human body, I can't dole it all out at once. I'll be helping one kid with something, and the other one will hook me into a conversation. Pretty soon I am letting them both down. The one who feels the most slighted will usually pick a fight with the other one, and sometimes they come to blows.

"One approach I used to use was to yell at the attacker and make him feel bad about himself for starting a fight. But that was ridiculous, because he was already feeling terrible about himself—or he wouldn't have picked the fight in the first place. I could not possibly make him feel any worse. One morning at breakfast, my sons were about to kill each other because I had mistakenly given one of them the last frozen waffle. I knew this was not simply about waffles. I made them leave the table and sit on the living room floor on either side of me. I told them that they were really mad at *me*, not each other, and they needed to understand that even though there were no waffles left in the box, I really loved them both very much. But, I explained to them, sometimes, in the morning, it is all I can do to toast breakfast.

"I thought of the most poignant line in the Torah, when poor Esau, re-alizing his brother has stolen his blessing, cries, 'Father, have you but one blessing?' My kids seem so worried that there won't be enough blessings for all of them. And the truth is, I sometimes feel worried too. Not about the waffles. But *do* I really have enough love to go around? Or, rather, enough energy to give out all the love?"

Perhaps we parents would judge ourselves less harshly if we acknowl-edged that we are not expected to love perfectly, equally, endlessly. That we are human beings, not God. God is the parent with infinite love for all God's children. We are merely parents who love our kids deeply but im-perfectly, doing our best to raise them to love each other—*and* to get out of the house on time in the morning.

PART 2

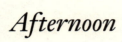

Afternoon

Chapter 5

COMMUNITY

Belonging

*"In my invented religion there are no services—
just announcements and refreshments."*

There is an old folk expression (I've heard both Africans and Jews take the credit) that says, "It takes a whole village to raise one child." Life was difficult for the people who coined that phrase, whoever they may have been, but one aspect was easy. They knew where their village was and who lived there. For some of us, finding a village to help us raise our children is a long, difficult task. By the time my older daughter was in kindergarten, she hesitated to volunteer at her new Hebrew school for a role in the upcoming play, fearing that by the time it was performed we might no longer belong to that synagogue. (We *had* switched around a lot.) Fortunately, our search ended at that point. But during those years of synagogue hopping, I learned a painful lesson: there is nothing less spiritual than being in a "sacred place" that evokes nothing sacred for you. And there is nothing lonelier than being with people who are a community for each other but not for you.

Hard as it is to find the right one, community—whether gathered around a religious tradition, a political cause, or a passionate interest—is enormously helpful in the spiritual journey of parenting. The Talmud puts it more strongly. At one point, a rabbi exclaims, *"O hevruta, o metuta,"* which loosely translated means "Give me a community or give me death!" The values and the faith we glimpse when we are alone or with our family take on substance when we congregate in a special place with others.

When I was still a rabbinical student, I learned a profound lesson about community, not from my professors at the seminary but from my congregants in my student pulpit. In my last years of rabbinical school, I traveled every Saturday morning to the Upper East Side of New York City to lead services for a group of well-heeled, liberal Jews. Most of them had learned the prayers we were saying together long before I was born.

When it snowed, my congregants, many of whom were over eighty, would all show up! When I expressed surprise, they explained that they did not want to disappoint the rest of the group. For me, part of a generation that regarded religion as something designed to meet *our* needs, this was a startling concept. More incredible was our congregational meeting about Anna, a mentally ill, homeless Jewish woman who had somehow discovered our services. She regularly wandered in with her shopping bags to sit in the back row and talk to herself. She smelled bad, was occasionally disruptive, and made me more nervous than I already was in my new job. I assumed that we would find a way to get her to stop coming. But several of the congregants would not hear of it. They recalled Robert Frost's "Home is the place where, when you have to go there, they have to take you in." A religious community is a home. Anna was a part of our extended family, and we would have to find a way to stretch to include her. So we did.

Many people told me that when they were young adults they had been very much on their own, dropping in and out of institutions and groups as their needs required. Then they became parents. As one father put it, "All of a sudden, I wanted to feel nailed down."

Raising children can be a lonely endeavor, even with a partner. I knew this from my own experience, and talking to Gail reinforced it. Gail had been a Roman Catholic nun for eleven years when she met Bill, a monk, at a summer computer institute. They enjoyed long strolls and deep conversations together. As their friendship grew, they noticed that the other students seemed to leave them alone as they took their evening walks. After everyone on campus knew that they were in love, Gail and Bill finally figured it out too. After much soul searching, they both wrote to the pope and their superiors and asked to be released from their vows.

When I interviewed Gail, I was interested in her transition from nun to mother. Did she miss the hours devoted to prayer and contemplation?

Gail's answer surprised me. "The main thing I missed when I became a mother was community. Both Bill and I were used to living in communities where there were many people around to pitch in and help out. The sisters and brothers all took responsibility when there was a task at hand. All of a sudden we had a job to do that ultimately was the responsibility of just the two of us. It felt lonely. When Bill was overwhelmed with work and errands and child care, I wanted to support him, but I also wished I wasn't doing it alone. When I needed Bill's help and he gave it, then I wished someone was there helping him."

A family is supported by being part of a group of families, a unit larger than itself. That support is physical—a hand to help, a meal cooked, a child driven somewhere—and it is also spiritual.

First, a community helps parents to teach values. Values are stronger if they are backed up by a group, particularly one with a tradition behind it. Jane is the daughter of a very conservative Protestant minister in the Midwest. She went to church every Sunday morning and evening and every Wednesday afternoon for the first eighteen years of her life. She recalls sitting in church and removing her mother's rings and sliding them on her fingers and then back on her mother's hands. She remembers nothing of the service, but she thinks she got something important "just by going." "I did not resent it any more than I resented brushing my teeth. We just did it. Even when it lost its meaning, it still had meaning. Eighteen years of my life—but I don't feel all those hours were wasted, not at all."

While nothing of the content of her parents' faith "took," she believes there was power in the way she was raised. "It gave me depth. There was something important I learned in that rigor and routine." What Jane took from her religious rearing were passion and discipline. Now she lives in California, a politically and religiously progressive Jew. "I met a liberal rabbi in Kansas," she explains, "who looked me in the eye and said he couldn't even promise me that there was a God. I knew right away that was the religion for me!" But Jane doesn't regret her hours in church. She now applies those qualities of character she learned as a child to the very different religious life she has chosen. Unlike many in her generation, she comes regularly to the services at her ultraliberal synagogue.

Jane sits with her daughter on her bed each night without fail and talks to her about her day. Sometimes they sing together, often choosing a favorite song they both enjoy singing in synagogue. It is based on a two-thousand-year-old teaching of Rabbi Hillel.

> *If I am not for myself, who will be for me?*
> *But if I am only for myself, what am I?*

One night they were discussing the day's events and Jane was trying to help ten-year-old Sarah see that she needed to help out more around the house. Jane began to sing quietly, "If I am not for myself, who will be for me?" Her daughter spontaneously joined in with the words "If I am only for myself, what am I?"

It was a magical moment. "I wasn't lecturing or inculcating a value," says Jane. "I drew it out of *her*. It had been put in there by the tradition, by the community, not by me. This value came out of her mouth and met itself coming out of my mouth. At that moment, it became real. We both looked at each other in amazement. I could have taught her about selfishness without having someone else teach her that song, but it wouldn't have been nearly as profound."

Second, a community provides people. By growing up with other people, we learn about the varieties of human nature and the vagaries of human existence. For many reasons, households today are smaller than they have ever been, and extended families are more geographically scattered. When I was young, each of my parents had many aunts and uncles. Social life revolved around relatives visiting our home. Although they were all Jewish, there the similarities ended. Some were very old and some were very young, some were poor and some were rich. Aunt Lena was one step above homeless, while Uncle Joe bought a new Cadillac every other year. Some of my relatives were smart and some were not. And things happened in an extended family. People were born, people died. Life, we learned, went on. An old saying has it that a house is not a home until there has been a birth, a death, and a wedding in it. These days, few people live in the same home from birth to death, and even fewer are born at home, marry at home, or die there. Our communities become our homes.

In our society, where expressions of sadness and grief are generally unwelcome, a community can be a safe place to mourn, a receptacle for messy feelings that at best are only tolerated in other institutions. When I asked Howard, who grew up in a small town in South Carolina, how he understood death as a small child, he said his religious community was a huge help, but not through the formal curriculum. When his Sunday school teacher's sister—a young mother—died of leukemia, the whole class went to the funeral. People cried and screamed at a loud pitch.

Howard recalled, "Afterward, everyone went back to the teacher's house with her family. Children were running about, yelling and laughing. Great quantities of food were consumed. All of life—the pain, the vitality, the absurdity—seemed to come together." Howard began to understand that loss, even a very terrible one like that of a young woman, was something that happened and that people survived it.

"The place was full of people from the church, and everyone belonged there. The minister spoke and gave everybody permission to be however they needed to be. He told the children, 'You know what it is like to have a little sister. Well, your teacher's little sister died, and it is a very sad thing.' Crying did not mean losing face. But running around happily and being a kid were also allowed. We kids knew that coming to the house had helped our teacher, and we felt good about ourselves for being there."

Community can offer the gift of acceptance. A good community, in the words of Mr. Rogers, "likes you just the way you are." For Joan, who is African-American, her church was a place where she could be safe from the racism outside. People fussed over her there. Even though she didn't like Sunday school, she still has every one of her textbooks, with her name written on the inside cover, neatly stacked on a shelf. "It was my home and they were my family."

Janice joined a synagogue mainly for "the sake of the children." Janice was surprised to discover how good she felt in that community. As a child, she had found going to synagogue a trial; she was certain she would say or do the wrong thing. "The funny thing is," she said, "I joined to give my kids a place to hang their hat, and I was the one who got hooked."

Each Friday night during services, a different woman lit the candles. When Janice first began to attend, she noticed that all the women would cover their eyes just before they recited the blessing. But in her childhood home, her grandmother and mother never covered their eyes. They extended their arms in front of them, palms down, as they faced the candles.

So when it is was her turn to go up in front of the whole congregation, that is what she did.

"My daughter was outraged!" Janice said. "She complained that no one else did it that way. I explained to her that this was *my* way. I like these people and they like me, so it doesn't matter. As I was explaining it, I realized what a gift she had given me by providing me with a motive for joining the synagogue. I had feared a religious community precisely because I didn't want to be judged. But I had discovered a community that said, Come as you are." Community, when it is doing its job well, helps us to experience in a very immediate way the more abstract claim of faith that God "accepts us as we are."

You may have noticed that all my examples so far involve religious communities. This reflects my bias—an occupational hazard of the clergy.

Religious communities do have certain strengths. Community in the context of a religious tradition can often be transferred from one place to another. Nora said, "We were always moving when my kids were young. But wherever we moved, we knew we would join the Presbyterian church; the kids would already know all the hymns, and soon we'd feel at home again." Almost everyone I know has said at some point, "I can pray better in the woods than in a building." But communities that are housed in buildings also have their role.

Karen, for example, experienced the church building as a repository of meaning when she was young. Later, it stood ready to serve that role again when she needed it as a parent. She had grown up in a devout Catholic family. She loved the church and the people she worshiped with every Sunday. She remembers driving in the car with her mother on weekday afternoons and passing their church. "Let's make a visit!" her mother would sometimes say. They would park the car, go into the empty sanctuary, get down on their knees in the silence, and pray for a few minutes. Karen always felt those were special times of connection with God. The walls held messages, left over from all that had happened within that space.

When Karen got older she stopped going to church because she objected to so many of the official policies. But she never stopped talking to God in her own way. As a mother with four children, she taught each of them to pray to God "like a friend who wants to hear your every secret," but she did not even consider having them baptized or taking them to religious services. Then her seven-year-old son, Brian, was diagnosed with cancer. During the last three years of his life, she spent many nights awake—wiping his brow after a surgery, reading to him, singing to him, lying in bed and worrying while he slept. "The thought that wouldn't let go of me was that I had brought him into this world and now he was suffering. I was the parent, the one who was responsible for him being here, the one who was supposed to take care of him, and I couldn't do anything to stop his pain and eventual death. I wanted to do everything I could for him—all the treatments, macrobiotic diet, support groups. Finally, I realized I also needed to feel I was in someone else's hands." She also seemed to need something more than the woods.

One day, she simply walked into the Catholic church nearest to her home, hundreds of miles from the church she had attended as a child. Immediately she was in touch with all her old feelings of contact with God—feelings left over from her spontaneous childhood visits. During the three years between her son's diagnosis and his death, Karen went to mass every Sunday.

In addition, on Tuesday nights she and Brian went to a charismatic prayer group in the basement of the church. Most of the other participants were elderly women. They would join hands in a circle with Brian in the center and pray for his healing. "For Brian, it felt like he was surrounded by warmth and light. He loved it, and it helped him get through the painful treatments. He was even baptized." When Brian died, they held a funeral for him in that church, and all the women from the group attended, along with many other relatives and friends. Karen knew that she had not been alone after all. She felt held both by others and by God. After the funeral, Karen went back to the church a few more times, but all she could do was cry. "Now, my family and I pray at home, but I don't think that will be the end of our story."

This same point was made by a father with whom I spoke who had opted out of religious community. This man is an anthropologist who has spent seven of the last twenty years living with primitive tribes. His children, who were raised before his fieldwork days, had no religious affiliation in their youth. "If I had it to do over again," he said, "I would rethink how we created their sense of community. We relied heavily on their school, which seemed to offer a strong social network in which to live our lives—people to whom we felt responsible and on whom we could rely for support. But when our kids went away to college, they didn't seem to know how to reconnect. My fieldwork has made me realize how different life is for people who know they have a place in the world where they belong. I call it 'psychological Blue Cross.' I wish I had given my kids a sense of being part of something bigger than their school."

For some parents, the problem with religious community is the public worship. "I don't believe the words in the prayer book, so how can I attend services, much less force my kids to do it?" But what goes on in a house of worship during services is only partly about the words in the prayer book. Parents often discover this because they don't always get to hear the words.

When Sam's son was a baby, he would take him to synagogue and hold him in his arms for the duration of the service. Sometimes he held the book, sometimes not, but he found being there with his child one of the most powerful worship experiences he'd ever had. Later, forced into the hallways by his toddler's need to run around, Sam found himself without book in hand, watching little children as he heard the prayers from the next room. Sometimes he would just set up shop in the hall right from the start.

Why didn't he just stay home? It was still important to him to be under the same roof with others who had come at the same time to touch base with what was deepest in themselves. His own prayers, often unspoken, were enriched by the prayers of others nearby. The words in the book mattered least of all.

As for children, I gather that boredom is not the worst thing that can happen to them. One woman I spoke with never attended any public religious events until she was in college. As a child, each year she would watch the Christmas mass on television enviously, fantasizing that she had a place in the worshiping throng. She longed to be part of something so beautiful and grand. As she put it, "I think I had a hole in my psyche, a God-shaped hole." Another told me that she went to Catholic mass almost every day with her grandmother. "I could not understand what was being said, but I was definitely inoculated for life. I have changed my beliefs and practices many times, but my deepest faith, an absolute conviction about the existence of Spirit, has never left me."

But there is also the other side. For some people, traditional religious institutions simply don't work. Beth, for example, divorced her husband shortly after learning that he had abused each of their children. After hearing the whole story, the rabbi of their Orthodox synagogue made it clear that he did not believe Beth's story, that her husband was still welcome as a member of the community, but that she was not. Beth finds community in other contexts now.

Marta Sanchez is a social worker in a program for pregnant women on medical assistance. She sits down with each of her clients and helps them map out their support systems on paper. "I always ask about the church," Marta said, "and sometimes the women agree that it is part of what supports them. But often, they look blank. 'What do you mean, support? Does the minister pay my rent?' Many of my clients think of the church as another institution that has failed them. When the church helps them with the real challenges of their lives like food and child care, then it begins to be a community for them."

Meg describes herself as a "recovering Catholic." Missing community, she decided to take her six-year-old, Lori, to the local Unitarian church on Christmas Eve. Meg loved hearing the familiar Christmas carols as the room grew darker and night fell. When they began lighting candles, Meg was in heaven. At that moment, Lori tugged at her mother's sleeve. Meg turned to see her daughter's face in the glow of the candlelight; Lori looked like a little angel. Meg leaned over to listen to Lori, imagining she was about to utter one of those sweet and profound comments you tell people about for years to come. "Mom," Lori said, "I was thinking I'd like to get Cheese Doodles on the way home." Meg realized that she needed to search for a community that touched both their souls; she eventually discovered it in a wonderful adult and child choral group.

In researching this book, I met many people like Meg. They showed me the variety of communal contexts in which families find spiritual nurture. The person who spoke most passionately and eloquently about the function of community in her spiritual life, for example, was someone who had found it in her urban neighborhood.

"My neighborhood isn't just people living on a block; it is a community. When one of us sees someone who looks unfamiliar in someone else's backyard, we call the police. Sometimes it turns out to be someone's father-in-law and we all have a good laugh, but it's worth erring on the side of caution. We protect each other. Last fall we all decided to enlarge the tree pits on our block, and then together we planted five hundred bulbs. We are constantly having block cleanups. During one of the terrible snowstorms, I called everyone on the street and told them to bring whatever they were cooking and come for dinner. We didn't choose each other, but now we support each other. Since I've lived on this block, two people have died, and I saw them carry the bodies out of the house. Four babies were born, and I watched them carry the little ones in. When I'm sick, my neighbors do my shopping. I will put it bluntly: I consider it a spiritual experience to pick up garbage on my block."

Why? What does all this have to do with a spiritual life? Let me paraphrase what I heard from this young mother: "Life is a series of concentric circles of connection. I am connected to myself, then to my family, then to my community, then to my city, my country, the earth, and finally to God. If a step is missing along the way, it makes the rest of the connections more difficult. As passionately as I feel about my family, I need to also have that passion about a larger group of people. As much as I love humankind, I have to love a smaller group first. For me, the connecting circle between my family and God is the neighborhood in which I live."

The operative word is *belonging*. Belonging to a community is an experience that helps us believe that we also belong in the universe, belong to God. Lois received this gift through her child. While she was pregnant, Lois watched with envy as her next-door neighbor—who had just had a baby—would answer the door to pots and pots of soup from her church friends. Lois looked around for a religious community but found all the churches near her home to be smug and self-satisfied. She was not sure about her own beliefs anyway, and she sensed these places would not welcome her doubts. Then her first child was born with Down syndrome.

Within a short time, Lois had found her community. She organized a group of mothers of children with Down syndrome that met weekly. Soon these people began to care for each other, support one another through life's passages, and mediate love for one another.

"How ironic!" Lois reflected. "The so-called tragedy of having a child with special needs was really a gift in this respect." It led Lois and her family to discover a life shared with others, without worry about creedal correctness. And the irony deepens. Through that community, Lois began to learn faith in a God of acceptance and love—an entirely new belief for her. "One day, my son was sick and three women from my group came by with food. All of a sudden, I remembered my neighbor with the pots of soup. I laughed! I had gotten the soup I had hoped for, and a whole lot more as well." Through the experience of belonging, Lois experienced God. She summed it up: "At this point I honestly *could* join a church, but now I don't need to, at least not for the reasons I originally thought."

Susan was overwhelmed with four children under the age of eight. She went to a church, but that wasn't where her deepest connections were found. She knew she had some good friends out there in the world, seven or eight women who lived in different parts of town whom she could count on in a crunch. It was they who gave meaning to her life, provided her with whatever sense she had of being held and upheld. But most of these women didn't know each other. One day, when Susan was feeling particularly exhausted, she suddenly realized that it would help her to feel supported if she had a community. So she decided to build one for herself. She invited her friends to meet once a month and share their lives through talk. The group became a community for one another, a source of sustenance for each of the members. The sharing in the group became Susan's primary religious experience. Motherhood had awakened in Susan the need; community had filled it.

I encountered more than one couple who bonded so fully with the people in their childbirth preparation class that after sharing that intense experience, they went on to meet regularly—with the now born children—and create a community in which to raise them. Some mothers discover in a nursing mother's class or group the raw material for a community of support that continues long after the children have stopped feeding at the breast.

So the last word is not a plug for religious community. Rather, it is an observation that serious community, in whatever form it appears, is inherently religious. And it is remarkably the same, in its essence, all over the world. Jacob raised his child in the intense communal structure of the Old Order Amish. He told me about his daughter's experience in life. The family left the Amish world when Rebecca was twelve. She attended public high school and then college. Later, as a member of the Peace Corps, she found herself far from Lancaster County, Pennsylvania, in a small village in Africa, in a different terrain and climate, speaking a foreign language and eating strange foods. Rebecca's first letter to her parents from Africa was short and to the point: "I feel completely at home." When Jacob interpreted that missive, what he learned was this: the village Rebecca was living in was a true community, an experience she knew from her child-hood. The particulars of time and place differed, but the essence was constant.

One of my young informants, a thirteen-year-old girl, told me that after being exposed to a variety of religious services, she invented her own religion. It was the essence of simplicity. "God created the world and that's it. You die and that's it. It doesn't matter what you wear to the services. Actually, there are no services, just the announcements and the refreshments."

This girl may not have gotten all that religion has to offer yet, but she has begun to appreciate sharing life with others. As she gets older, she will find that she was right not to leave community out of her invented religion. For many, the home a community offers is a profound glimpse of grace. As Robert Frost said about home,

> *I should have called it*
> *Something you somehow haven't to deserve.*

Chapter 6

PLAYTIME

Character

*"We'll always love you, but we want to
raise you so other people will love you too."*

In Yiddish, the word *mensch* literally means "human being." It connotes quite a bit more. A mensch is someone who acts with integrity, someone who is responsible, who is decent and fair and honest. Another Yiddish word, *edelkeit*, complements it. *Edelkeit* means nobility of soul. A person possessing *edelkeit* is compassionate, loving, generous of spirit. When I asked parents what they wanted for their children, this is what they told me—those few who knew Yiddish and the great majority who did not: "I want my child to be a person who radiates *edelkeit*. I want my child to be a mensch."

When playtime comes, the little mensch in training is brought to the playground, carrying his beloved ball. The parent watches from the bench, pretending to be interested in the other parents' gossip, really interested in the child. When someone else wants to play with the ball, what will he do? Will he display the *edelkeit* I have tried so hard to instill? Will he be the mensch I so want him to be? Or will he push the other child into the sandbox? And then comes the question that makes parenthood the spiritual journey it is. If he doesn't act as I hoped, will I be a mensch? Or will I push *him* into the sandbox?

The challenge of shaping our children's character is a spiritual education for us. Sometimes, children's innate goodness startles their parents and evokes their awe. Just as often, however, parents are shocked and frustrated by their child's crabby, selfish, or even violent nature. Parents discover anew the underside of humanity. And in their response to their child's character flaws, parents find darkness in their own hearts. Yet they also discover, again to their surprise, that their desire to be better parents sometimes pushes them to become better people.

The depth of compassion we sometimes see in our children hardly feels natural. Rather, it seems almost supernatural. Every parent has his or her special memories, moments that ripped them open with emotion. Jeremy told me one that had us both in tears by the end. "I took my two daughters to a new swimming pool. Although the older one could swim, the younger one could not. The little one was sitting on her sister's shoulders and being carried around the shallow end, her legs held down by her sister's hands. Suddenly, without realizing it, the older one walked further into the pool, too deep to stand. I watched from a distance as, terrified, my daughter surveyed her options: ditch her sister and swim or try to keep her sister up while slowly sinking herself.

"I watched my daughter resolutely try to tread water with just her feet. While both hands held tightly to her sister's legs, the water covered her face and eventually submerged her. By then, I was in the water and could pull the little one off to safety so the older could swim up to the surface. She was frightened but unharmed. I could not get over it. *Where did that come from?* I wondered. I tried to teach her basic rules and values, but this came from someplace else. She had just risked drowning rather than abandon her sister. I did not know there was as much love in my soul as I felt that day for my daughter."

Rona wanted to teach her daughter about the spark of divinity in every human being, but her daughter ended up teaching her. "When my daughter was only five, we were walking through the supermarket, and a mentally ill man started following us. He clearly wanted to relate to us. My instinct was to walk faster, lose him. My daughter turned and began to chat with him. He seemed delighted and proved to be harmless. Afterward we discussed this at length. I explained my position: I didn't understand this man, and I was afraid of him. The best course in such a situation is to steer clear. My daughter explained her position: we did not know for sure what he was like; he could not harm us in a supermarket, so why not give him a chance?

"I realized I had become hardened by life, while she still believed the principles I preached. There *is* divinity in every human being. How am I supposed to teach *her* goodness? I could teach her prudence; she could teach *me* goodness."

Yet there is the other side. Some parents were struck by how difficult it is to become a mensch—how much darkness lurks just under the surface. Civilization is a thin veneer. Winnie found that when she could acknowledge her son's wilder instincts, it was easier to teach him how to manage them.

"One day Fred, who was about eight, wanted something very badly— I can't recall what—and I said no. He was so furious he began to lash out at me. I told him he was not permitted to hurt me. He began to curse and yell. I told him he was not permitted to curse. He was beside himself with rage. He asked for whatever it was again. Again, I said no. He looked like he would shoot me if there had been a gun. I told him that I knew he felt angry and asked him if anything could make him feel better. What did he most feel like doing? He said he would like very much to spit at me.

"I was totally disgusted by this idea, but I had to admit that it was completely honest. He was also now under control and waiting respectfully for permission. Yes, he was tremendously angry, but he was learning that most of the ways he felt like acting when he was angry were forbidden to him. He was successfully controlling the impulse to indulge in them. I said it would be OK, just this time, for him to spit at me. Once. He spat. With an elaborate flourish, I wiped my cheek and said, 'Yuck!' At that point, we both burst out laughing. It was over.

"I felt great. I was teaching him mastery over his antisocial instincts while acknowledging that they existed. For a long time, I could not do that because I was too upset by them. When I see them as human, part of our flawed nature (we are not gods, after all), then every once in a while, under very controlled circumstances, like the spit, I can even honor them."

Teaching children to become better people is a chance for us to grow. Sometimes what we call children's "behavior problems" are there to teach us something. The story is told about a monastery that included one very difficult man who fought with others constantly. Finally, the man left. The spiritual leader of the community pursued the man and convinced him to return to the community by paying him a salary. The monks were outraged. Why bring this man back at all, and why *pay* him on top of it?

The leader explained, "This man helps you learn about patience, about compassion. That is why I hire him." Maybe our children's difficult behavior is just so we can learn what we need to know.

Anger is a huge problem for parents; many report that they grow as human beings when they learn how to transcend it. Fran said, "When my husband and I first had children we discussed the issue of punishment. We agreed that we would never physically punish a child unless the child was about to put her finger in an electric outlet or run into a street filled with traffic. But as my kids got older, I found myself getting into battles with them constantly over the littlest things. Once I drew a line in the sand, I felt I had to stick by my demands, just to show them who was in control. The problem was that they didn't listen, and it made me so angry I got *out* of control, often whacking them on the bottom.

"When my daughter was five or six, she began to speak in a very flip way to me, something she must have picked up in school. On two or three occasions, I very consciously slapped her on the face. I began to feel a lot of remorse about those slaps. It seemed to me it was a serious violation of who she was as a person. I began to believe that it was abusive to hit someone who is vulnerable, dependent on you. I made a resolve to never slap or even whack again. But I had no idea if I could keep it.

"I began a prayer life that consisted of one request: gift me with calm, teach me a better way to deal with all this. I needed to contact a higher force within me from which to teach my children mutual respect. Over the years, through lots of work and meditation and prayer, I found it.

"That whole experience actually deepened my sense of what it means to be a moral person, acting in a spiritually aware and conscious way. I set for myself a norm that I have kept; in ten years, I have not touched one of my children in anger. It meant a lot for my own evolution as an adult to see that I could set that kind of standard for myself, be clear about my reasons, and then stick to it."

Bill grew up on spankings, but he never felt they were abusive. "My Dad would always hug us first and say, 'We love you no matter what you do, but that won't be true out there in the world. We have to make you the kind of person *other* people will love as well. I'm going to spank you now, but only to prevent someone else from doing it first.'" Bill loved his father and respected his child rearing, and he knew the biblical verse "Spare the rod, spoil the child." But Bill had no intention of spanking his children, and he never did. "I decided that in biblical times, a rod was an instrument shepherds used to guide the sheep down the path. So I reinterpreted the verse to mean direction, not physical punishment."

Parents often struggle with the relationship between religion and moral education. Martin grew up in a very tightly knit Christian community about an hour outside of Philadelphia. He married a woman who also grew up in the church; both of them swore they would never live in that town again. They moved to the city and loved its diversity of opinions and activities. They pursued their careers, made friends, and developed themselves as human beings, including learning about themselves through therapy. Neither of them ever stopped believing in God or in "bettering ourselves through spiritual principles."

When their two small children were ready for school, they felt that they were being "pulled home." Martin explained, "We wanted our children growing up among people with whom they could talk about God and not be embarrassed." Martin and his wife and children now live in their hometown, just minutes from their parents and childhood friends.

For Martin's parents, discipline and faith had a clear connection: parents were God's representatives to their children; their role was to teach the children right from wrong and to administer punishments. Their job was to remind their children of what God wanted of them. Martin sees it differently: "When my children are misbehaving, I am often tempted to invoke God. I know my kids believe deeply in God, and it would be easy to say to them, 'The Lord does not want you to be doing that.' But that feels too heavy. It is really *me* who does not want them to be doing whatever they are doing. I don't want to hit them over the head with spirituality as a weapon to be used when I am angry. I would rather talk about God when my kid comes to me feeling vulnerable, asking me to help him figure out a problem. I say to him, 'You know you can talk to God about that.' The way I was brought up, God mainly came into the picture to enforce rules. I am trying to take on more of the discipline myself and save God as a source of inspiration and support."

Marie said that for her, discipline is a constant battle between the side of her that just wants to shower her children with love and the side that wants to teach them limits. Her son is tucked into bed, and then he comes back out and asks for her to lie by his side till he falls asleep. No special reason, he just likes it. She actually likes it too. But there is a rule that bedtime must be observed. He needs to learn to sleep by himself, to follow the procedures. So she marches him back upstairs, gives him a big kiss and hug, and then sits on the living room couch by herself in torment.

Marie thinks to herself, "I love him so much I want to just give him every bit of nurturing he needs. But sometimes I make life hard for him, because I think it makes sense to teach him. So I sit on the couch and just think about all this and try to learn from it something about my own life. I want God to be lying by my side all the time, hugging me, but maybe sometimes she's sitting downstairs on a couch teaching me how to do things for myself."

Wendy had studied psychology in college and had been very critical of behavior modification. She had to write a whole paper about B. F. Skinner, and it was entirely negative. She believed she would inculcate desirable traits and behaviors in her children through more profound methods. But midway in her career as a parent, philosophy and theory started to matter less than results. "Every time we went anywhere in the car, my kids fought. Badly. It was making me crazy. Finally, I did what I had always vowed I'd never do. I went to a two-session seminar on child rearing. The teacher suggested a marble jar, with marbles added each time the desired behavior was manifest and subtracted when bad behavior set in. When the jar was full: a prize! It seemed shallow, but I was ready to try anything.

"I made up my version of the marble jar. It was called Warm Fuzzies. We put a glass jar in a prominent place in the kitchen. Every time the children made it through twenty minutes together without a squabble, one warm fuzzy (a cotton ball) would go into the jar. When the jar was completely full, they could get Nintendo. The children adored this system, and they fought less and less. When the jar was full, we bought the promised prize. Three days later, they had lost interest in the Nintendo. They had also lost interest in the jar. But the children were clearly fighting much less; the good behavior had become a habit. So I learned a lesson that helped me in my own life: good actions, whatever the motivation, create their own momentum. I became an Aristotelian."

Karen noticed that the difference between moralism and real moral teaching was the spiritual base from which she spoke. "I used to give little lectures to my kids on moral topics. But they would get to the point where they would just laugh and say, 'Here comes Mom's lecture number 342!' After I started going to church and feeling more deeply the spiritual basis of my own desire to be a good person, I kept giving lectures but they were coming from a different place. The children seemed to notice. Now when I see them wasting food, I might stop them and say, 'This isn't kind. You need to stop this and look at it.' I share with them why waste hurts me and hurts God, as I understand it. They know I am talking from my heart, and they actually listen to the lecture now."

Children sometimes motivate us to discipline ourselves. My oldest child forced me to begin working on one of my worst moral failings, gossip. (I am sorry to report that one of the places I became accomplished in this "skill" was the play group I attended when my children were little. In retrospect, I can see that the boredom, sense of impotence, and narrowing of horizons of early parenthood were just the conditions in which gossip could flourish.)

I knew this was a failing, but it was not until my twelve-year-old daughter and I attended a study session together on the subject of "bad speech" in the Jewish tradition that I finally got serious about weaning myself from this habit. During that session my daughter told me how much my failings in this realm hurt her. All the sermons I had heard (and even given!) on the topic were not nearly as effective as that simple statement from my own child. I thought about the ways I had tried to train my daughter in good paths, looking for one that would help me. Finally, I hit on an idea I had seen years ago in the home of a friend. Since I did most of my gossiping on the telephone, I pasted a reminder on the handle of each phone, a verse from Proverbs that says, "On her lips was kindness."

Sandra told me, "Before I had kids, I never worked on myself. I grew up in California and rejected all that stuff about processing feelings and going to therapy. But when my kid was in pain, I knew that she was carrying around some weighty stuff, and I knew, too, that I had put it there. The only way to get it off her back was for me to do some serious digging around in my own psyche. So I did. And it was a good thing for me."

Howard was divorced and his twelve-year-old son, Max, had just come to live with him full time. One night, they had a huge fight, and Max was threatening to get his baseball bat and hit his father. Howard did not know what to do next. "I was out of my depth. I knew in another minute, I would be the one heading for that bat. Suddenly, I remembered something I had heard two weeks earlier at a seminar I attended at work. It was a human relations training for salespeople at my company. The leader told us that usually people are most difficult when they are most in need of positive attention. He suggested that when dealing with hard-to-manage customers, we should be *especially* nice, even complimentary. So I turned to my raging son and said, 'Max, I love you very much. You are a good kid.' It was like magic! The whole situation turned around. I learned something very important that day, not only about dealing with business customers or even with Max but about the way life works."

Sometimes it takes laughter to help us through tough spots. If we can laugh, we can learn to see the absurdity of our own situation. Humility is the hard-won reward. Johanna started yelling one night and just could not stop. She screamed, "Do you know what makes me mad? You are doing the dishes all wrong. And do you know what else makes me mad? This house is a pigsty and no one seems to care but me. And on top of that, neither of you can manage to keep your elbows off the table, and you aren't doing really well on not fighting with each other, and . . . you know what *really* makes me mad? When I am yelling at you, my hair always falls in my eyes and I can't see anymore!" At that point, they all began to laugh, and the laughter dissipated the anger. "Within minutes," Johanna reported, "the kids were happily improving their behavior."

Occasionally, while parents are planning how to morally educate their child, the child goes off and discovers her own code. Both Les and his wife, Joan, grew up in liberal Jewish households with minimal observance. They now are living an Orthodox Jewish life in large part because of a conversion experience—not their own but that of their twelve-year-old daughter.

Les told me their story. "When Sarah was in sixth grade, she got very friendly with her Hebrew teacher, who happened to come from an Orthodox community in Israel. The teacher offered Sarah a two-month trip to Israel if she would act as a mother's helper. We packed a trunk full of shorts and T-shirts with one or two dresses and sent her off. Sarah's letters were vague, but when she got off the plane at the end of the summer, we knew something had changed.

"First, it was a hot day and she was wearing a long skirt and a long-sleeved shirt. When I unpacked her trunk, I saw that the shorts and T-shirts had been untouched. As she began to tell us about the summer in broken English (her Hebrew was better than her English at that point), we realized she had been totally engaged in a complete community, a thoroughgoing lifestyle, and she was now passionately committed to following it.

"What had appealed to her was the strong sense of moral values and purpose. She kept saying she felt more complete there. She found that the children at her school back home seemed superficial in comparison. In the apartment house in which Sarah lived in Israel, on Friday afternoon an old lady across the landing would yell out, 'I need someone to wash the floor for Shabbat!' A mother would inevitably send her son or daughter over with a mop. Sarah liked that feeling of connection and caring. She loved the structure. Knowing what was expected at all times made her feel safe.

"When she returned, we had to renegotiate many things as a family—how kosher the food in our home was, what we would do on the Sabbath. If we wanted to have an integrated family life, we needed to make some changes. We worked through many issues. Once Sarah made up her mind about her life's direction, she never wavered. She led the rest of us on a path. She had a level of discipline that encouraged us."

Not every set of parents would have reacted the way Les and his wife did. They saw their daughter's choice as one that had potential for them as well. Like so many parents (including me), they had been reluctant to impose too much structure on their daughter's life. They had given her a great deal of freedom. Their education about values had been ad hoc, rather than part of a tightly woven community with clear systems and norms. Now their daughter had used her freedom to opt for a detailed life plan in which values were embedded in specific rules and customs.

As a mother of a daughter on the verge of adolescence, I could not help envying Les's situation just a little. Many of the values Sarah has devoted herself to in choosing an Orthodox Jewish life are also my values. I wish there were a way for me to offer these values to my daughters in such an integrated and compelling fashion. On the other hand, there is too much of the Orthodox Jewish worldview that I do not share. For me, that kind of "conversion" would not work. Nevertheless, I think often of Sarah and wonder how we "freethinking" parents can also give our children a clear and coherent set of norms and structures that embody our values.

Gail is an ethicist by training. She now spends her days with her two young children in the playground. She wants to make her children kind and good. She spends all day with them, helping them through the little trials and joys of the sandbox. She models giving and sharing. She sees the hugest challenge as being how to evoke the behavior she wants from her children by the way she lives. She feels all these issues with great immediacy. Ethics is no longer abstract but something she does with her own hands.

When Gail was young, her mother taught her that "we are the hands of God to each other." Now each Saturday night when the blessing over light is recited to mark the end of the Sabbath, she follows the custom of extending her palms to the candle to catch its reflection. As she gazes at her outstretched hands, glowing a bit from the flame just beyond, she thinks to herself of her week ahead, of how she wants to be with her children, of the kindness she wants to teach them and the way in which she wants to do it. She whispers to herself, "These hands are God's hands. This week, may they do holy work."

Chapter 7

NAP TIME

Being Versus Doing

"What I liked best about being here was being here."

The parent of young children counts the minutes until nap time, that sacred space in the middle of the day when, if Roto-Rooter does not choose that hour to visit and there are not three phone calls to make and a stack of bills to pay, the parent might have some time to do . . . absolutely nothing. The pauses between the notes, the times of being rather than doing, the experience of resting are all critical to the spiritual journey of parenting.

Many of the people I interviewed were hardworking, highly successful professionals. Peggy had been so well into the groove of her professional track that she hardly missed a beat when her first child was born. "I took off two weeks for the birth and recuperation, and then hired a nanny and went back to sixty hours a week." Three years later, still working as hard as ever, she learned that her second pregnancy was in trouble. "The doctor said if I wanted the baby I would have to stay in bed for the next four months. I had never in my life done anything like that. But I wanted that child, so I did. And the most remarkable thing happened to me. I stopped in my tracks. Being in bed for four months changed my life. I lost some of my ambition and discovered some of my soul."

For some parents, the learning is a bit less dramatic. "I am so driven," said Mark, "and my time feels so precious, I hate to waste it. But making every minute have its agenda is a horrible way to live. Over the years, my kids helped me realize that. Since I did not want to model that drivenness for them, I slowed up a bit for their sake. It ended up helping me a lot."

Matthew confessed, "I had to work on just being there. If I walked into my daughter's room, there would always be a piece of duty involved: get her to clean her room, to write a thank-you note. I literally had to train myself to take the time to walk in there and just be with her. To sit down on her bed with nothing at all in mind. I finally got the hang of it."

Said Carol, "The great paradox for me in the parenting business is that I am intrigued by my kids just the way they are and I accept them with unconditional love, yet I always feel this need to keep working on them, to make them better, to fix them. I'm always inserting myself where I don't belong. But it is my job to raise them, which can't mean just accepting everything about them just as it is."

The resolution of the paradox is in balancing: there is a time for every purpose under heaven. A time to fix and a time to enjoy. A time for weekdays and a time for Sabbath. A time for work and a time for vacations. I always thought it was ironic that on the Sabbath, a time when we appreciate being rather than striving, the Jewish tradition has us bless our children by comparing them to their biblical forebears ("May God bless you like Sarah, Rebecca, Rachel, and Leah"). Why did they have to be blessed like somebody else? Shouldn't we simply congratulate them for being themselves? As a result, in our house we rewrote the blessing to say, "Thank you, God, for making Rena Rena." On weekdays we could work on improvements.

Lao-tzu once said, "What is important about a cup is the empty part inside." It is not only in the East that we find this wisdom. For the Western tradition, the holiest day of the week is the day when we are supposed to sit still and do nothing. The essence of the biblical idea of the Sabbath is that there is "no agenda." As Isaiah said, "in sitting still and rest shall ye be saved" (30:15). But how many of us believe it?

For many people today, the Sabbath has disappeared from life. Stores are open and E-mail is sent and received seven days a week. When a Hebrew school teacher I know instructed her class to ask their parents why they did not observe the Sabbath, each child came back with the same answer: "We do not have time." It was hardly a large sample, but the result seems accurate.

Parents today have barely enough time to *do* things with their children; doing nothing is clearly an extravagance. And yet, several parents confessed that they welcomed those occasions when they or their child got sick—not too sick, just sick enough to justify resting. My friend Debbie believes that if there were no such thing as Sabbath, yuppies would have had to invent it out of sheer physical and spiritual exhaustion.

Even those who do mark Saturday or Sunday as special often find this aspect of the Sabbath—doing nothing—entirely foreign. We appreciate the beauty and meaning in an active ritual like lighting candles or having a family meal or going to church. It is harder to understand the beauty and meaning of not accomplishing, not spending, not changing, not building, or not doing much of anything. Often, we reinterpret Sabbath. Since it is meant to help us remember the creation of the world, we engage in activities on the Sabbath that are creative or recreative.

There is much wisdom in that insight. Hiking, games, art projects, and visiting museums are all meaningful ways to participate in the creativity that was God's at the beginning of time. But there is also some value in remembering that the Sabbath does *not* commemorate the six days in which God created the world. The days of our workweek are our commemoration of that. The seventh day is the day God ceased from work and did *nothing*.

Two questions come to mind. How do you do nothing with children? And why? Let's begin with the second question. In his book on child rearing, Stanley Greenspan recommends as a tonic for just about every psychological ailment of childhood something he calls "floor time." Essentially, Greenspan insists to the educated, high-achieving, and overbusy parents who are his clientele that they must commit themselves to half an hour a day with their children in which they sit on the floor (with older children you can hang out in a fashion more comfortable for them) and *do nothing*. The instructions are very precise. Not only may you not plan to do anything specific, you may not even have any agenda at all.

Dr. Greenspan finds that parents are generally terrified by this suggestion, since they are used to budgeting time for their children carefully, with explicit plans and goals attached to each hour. But after a while, they come to love floor time. So do the children. What do the children do? Younger ones engage in imaginative dramatic play in which the parents are then drawn into the story. Older ones talk . . . or don't. But the important thing is that nothing is planned. By sitting still, you are saved.

Another child-rearing authority, Martha Welch, suggests a technique called "holding time": the parent commits to a daily time of physical contact with the child in which there is no program—no book to be read and listened to, no moral or spiritual lesson to be learned, no expectations. The child can vent all kinds of emotions verbally or in appropriate, permitted nonverbal ways. Any kind of feeling is permitted. The child is also free to do nothing at all and still get held.

Have these medically trained therapists rediscovered the essence of the Sabbath? And is it not a very significant message for today's overprogrammed children? It's OK to do nothing. It's OK to just be. Stanley Elkin said the children of today are getting too many lessons, too many schedules. Parents do the same thing to themselves. Sabbath, traditionally, is an opportunity for parents and their children to do the exact opposite of what they do the rest of the week—that is, to do nothing. The Jewish tradition calls the Sabbath a "pearl"—a precious gift. Perhaps it is even more so today, for we have so many more distractions and feel so much more driven to achieve.

Can children handle doing nothing, having no plans, or will they get bored? Boredom is actually something very wonderful, says author Frances Moore Lappé in a book about the virtues of the unplugged television set. Boredom forces you to dig in and find yourself.

Doing nothing isn't a newfangled psychological technique. It is the spiritual teaching of the East and the West. It carries with it a message central to the spiritual life: *you* are loved by God, not your book reports or your piano recitals or anything you accomplish. Just you. It's hard to teach that lesson unless you believe it yourself, yet few of us do. And this is where a rather wonderful circle comes into play.

Our children can teach us that lesson. Look how they love us just for being there! "The biggest surprise for me," said one mother, "was discovering how much my kids loved me. I had never felt so loved before. They gave me so many hugs for so many years, it really helped me to feel loved just for being who I was. And isn't it true, after all, that you love them just for being, even when they are doing nothing?"

Taking time to be rather than do is a way of asserting control by letting go. We are the masters of our own fate, our own time. We can say no to the phone, to technology, to work, to anything. This is the great gift of the Sabbath. My eleven-year-old daughter reminded me of this. When Seth and I were newly married graduate students, we committed ourselves to not doing any of our own work on the Sabbath. For the first twelve years we had children, it was hard to know what they thought of this practice, since their elementary school did not give any homework on weekends. When my older daughter began middle school, she was taught "study skills." The teacher handed out a schedule for the entire week with blank spaces where the students could fill in all their scheduled activities. Then in the boxes that were left over, they were to plot out homework times in which they could do their long-term assignments.

My daughter, who was feeling overwhelmed by all the new demands on her, felt like the school was crushing her spirit. She sat down with the schedule and drew a huge X across Friday evening and then another across Saturday morning and afternoon. She looked up with satisfaction and said, "I am not allowed to work at those times! It is Shabbat. And nobody can make me!" I wanted to shout, "Hurray! The law makes you free!" It is in our power to say no to relentless demands of time, to be masters of our fate enough to sanctify some hours of our week and make them holy. We can say that one-seventh of our lives can be set aside for our souls.

Having time off is also a way to put our values in perspective. Judy, who observes a traditional Jewish Sabbath, had an experience as a young mother that clarified for her what the Sabbath was all about. "One Friday night, it was very hot and we accidentally left some windows open when we went to sleep. The next morning, we came downstairs to discover that my pocketbook, which had been sitting out on the kitchen counter, was gone. I panicked. I knew my car keys had been in the pocketbook, so I raced outside to confirm my fear: the car was gone too. I had lost money, credit cards, a car, all these terribly important things. I raced to the telephone to start making my reports when I remembered that it was Shabbat. I was not permitted to use the telephone. But if I couldn't use the phone, I suddenly realized, I also couldn't use the car or the money or the credit cards either. So I took a deep breath, relaxed, and enjoyed the rest of the day, walking to synagogue, visiting with friends and family, exactly what we always do on Saturdays.

"After sunset, I called the police. But by then I had a whole different perspective on the situation. It was not the earth-shattering crisis I had thought when I first discovered the loss. Shabbat made me realize that everything that mattered most to me in the world was untouched by the robbery."

How do parents make Sabbath happen for themselves and their children? Those who live within a traditional community know the rules and simply follow them. For others, it is more of a creative art form. "I'm a single mother with a teenage son," said Ruth, "and I can't always get it together for a special meal on Friday night. Often, one or the other of us goes out. When we are home together, we certainly don't follow all the rules of the Sabbath. But we did want it to be special, so we sat down and made a contract with each other. For twenty-four hours, I would not talk on the phone and he would not watch TV. It's a special commitment we make to each other; the rest of the system gets observed in the breech rather than the practice."

Brian told me, "When our kids were little, we tried to institute a no-TV policy on the Sabbath for all the right reasons. Except the policy wasn't right. My son Gabe adored a particular TV show that came on Friday nights. So we decided instead to all watch it with him. My wife and I didn't even like the show, but we liked being a family together on Friday nights, and my son loved the fact that we all cared enough to watch his show with him. We would all get into a king-size bed and watch it together at 8:30 every Friday. Those are happy memories."

For many families, Sabbath is not a weekly practice, yet they do experience what it means to stop in the midst of life and just "be." Some allow their children to play hooky once or twice a year, a sanctioned "rest and relaxation" break, preferably with parents playing hooky too. For most families, the major experience of rest is vacations. Like the Sabbath, vacations are times to recreate our spirits, sanctuaries in time rather than space. Parents whom I interviewed often told me about vacations as time when they got a glimpse of the deeper meaning to their lives as parents. I heard about four kinds of vacations, each important in its own way to parents and children.

The first, and perhaps the most obvious, is the family vacation—a time when the entire family leaves their routine to live in a different place at a different pace. Families often find vacations are a time to connect with each other, to create memories. If members of the family can find activities they all enjoy, these times (even if they are very infrequent) become important glue. "At home, we all were busy living our parallel lives," Dan said. "On vacation we intersected. At first, the kids would ignore each other. Then they would fight. Then they would start to play together. Every year we went to the same lake for one week. We always rented the same cottage. The last night we always swam across the whole lake. The year our dog was dying, it was important that he make it to the lake for his final swim. Our family vacations were our sacred times."

(In fairness, I should report that there was a small but vocal minority who said that their family hated vacations. After many years, they finally accepted the fact that they loved each other but found vacations stressful and unrewarding. Some even had the courage to stop taking them.)

The second kind of vacation is also fairly obvious, although less frequent. Parents need time away together, without their children. These times of rest, of retreat, of just being rather than doing, are essential to nourish relationships that are often frayed by the stress of child rearing. It took me a long time to bring myself to do this, and longer still to do it without qualms and guilt (Seth says I still have not entirely achieved that goal). But part of the spiritual journey of parenting, when one has a partner, must be making sure the partnership survives the trip. The travelers need to stay in conversation.

Beth recalled, "We were doing so many things during the years our kids were young, we figured our relationship was at the bottom of the list. Then we saw friends starting to get divorced, and it scared us. So we went away for a weekend alone and remembered why we had gotten married and had all these kids in the first place. We made two pledges to each other after that vacation: first, we would each call the other once during each workday to check in. Second, we decided that during the Lord's Prayer in our weekly church service we would always hold hands. These two things have kept us connected."

David and his wife have never been able to afford vacations together. "We take the most extreme form of 'minivacation.' Three times a week we meet at the kitchen table at eleven at night and drink tea and talk for two hours or so. It's not glamorous, but it is our chance to recoup, and we look forward to it."

The third kind of vacation is one I first learned about from Sharon. It is a vacation taken by one parent with one child—a special time of connection, just the two of them. Sharon annually took each of her three children individually on a ski weekend. While I was impressed by the concept, it seemed to have little to do with my life—or, I suspect, with many of yours. Who can afford ski weekends, much less several a winter? Then I met Barbara, a single mother without much money, whose company sent her each year to a nearby city overnight. One year, when her teenage daughter Cathy was barely speaking to her, Barbara decided to invite Cathy to come along. "The offer was so unusual Cathy couldn't pass it up. At night, lying next to each other in the hotel room in the dark, we chatted about many topics. The next morning, Cathy looked at me with a look that said, 'Don't you dare mention what happened last night, and don't count on it happening again.' It did not. At least for a long while. But it was still a wonderful interlude."

When Greg took his six-year-old son on a camping trip, he thought it would be an opportunity for the two of them to connect. But at night in the dark tent, Greg's son began to cry. He missed his mother, Susan, and wanted to go home. Knowing it was impossible to hike out at night, Greg tried desperately to come up with something to allay his son's distress. Finally, he said, "Let's tell stories about what we like best about Mom." For the next forty-five minutes, father and son took turns telling each other things about Susan that they liked. "My son kept coming up with these wonderful statements like 'She makes me eat healthy food like oatmeal,' and each time I had to come up with something I loved about Susan. After a while, my son drifted off to sleep, and I just lay there in the dark—moved beyond measure—in tears." Ironically, a trip that was designed to make father and son feel close to each other also had the effect of intensifying the bonds they each had with the missing family member.

The last kind of vacation, the parent solo, is the one least thought about, least practiced, and perhaps most critical to the spiritual journey of parenting. Parenting is so interactive, there is always someone else around. As one mother put it, "spending a day with children offers a million occasions to say a blessing and almost no time to do so."

The idea of being entirely alone is one that appeals to many parents. I often heard mothers describe spending half an hour on the toilet only to realize that what they loved so much about the bathroom was the unique peace and solitude it provided. Chris told me that when her three sons were small, she used to stay up till they and their father were all soundly asleep. Then she would sit alone in the living room and play the same songs on the piano over and over again, singing her lungs out, until past midnight. "It replenished me. I got less sleep but more strength to face the morning."

Nell found her extensive prayer life was curtailed by children, but she always grabbed ten minutes by herself just before the "arsenic hour" (4:00

to 6:00 P.M.). She would sneak off to her room and pray alone. She wondered how other parents survive that grouchy time without such an interlude.

I searched to find parents who had actually gone on retreat alone while their children were young. Did they manage to do the work they needed to do, or did they spend the whole time worrying about what was going on back at home?

"When my kids were eight and three, I went away for a week and I rediscovered who I was besides a mother," Sonia recalled. "I missed them a lot, especially at bedtime when I couldn't perform the little rituals. But I remembered parts of myself I had forgotten. That was the benefit I expected. The biggest surprise was that being apart from my husband and kids made me feel more poignantly how deeply connected I was to them. When we were together every minute, I couldn't feel it as strongly. But when I was alone for the first time, it was really clear. I was part of something bigger than myself.

"When I came back, I just gloried in the kids. I had hoped that I would look forward to seeing them again ('absence makes the heart grow fonder'), but I was really surprised by how much I just wanted to be with them. I was genuinely curious to get to know them again. I was interested to hear their ideas, their questions. Who are these little people? I found them more fascinating because they seemed to be more like separate people from me, less like simply extensions of myself."

Rebecca, who is active in the Swedenborgian church, told me about retreats for mothers, weekends that literally saved her soul during the years she was raising small children. "We would go to the mountains, sometimes twenty women, sometimes as many as eighty, and spend two days talking about our lives. We slept on the floor in sleeping bags, cooked meals together, shared prayers, songs, meditations, even droning. We would all grow incredibly close. On Saturday night, we would turn on rock music and go crazy dancing all night. By late Sunday, we would be ready to return to our husbands and kids."

Back home, parents can use time caring for the children as time to grow spiritually. Alone with a child is a good time to try to be fully present, in the moment. For some parents, the relative solitude of parenting is a challenge. Seth remembers how strange it was to find himself all alone with his child for hours at a time. He quickly realized that no one would ever know if he propped a bottle in her mouth or held her in his arms and sang. Seth is a teacher, and he used to think of teaching as an unsung profession. He had always liked the line from *A Man for All Seasons* in which Sir Thomas More suggests to Richard that he would make a great teacher, and Richard objects, "And if I was, who would know it?" To which More responds, "You, your pupils, your friends, God. Not a bad public, that." That line kept coming back to him as he took care of his child alone. Who will ever know? "You, your child, God." As the months went on, he would remind himself, "Not a bad public, that."

Being present is not easy. I remember when I was a graduate student at Yale University hearing Rabbi Arnold Jacob Wolf counsel a Jewish student who could not decide whether to skip classes for the High Holiday services. "Go to class," the rabbi told him. "If you come to services, you will think about your class. If you go to class, you will think about the services. I want you to think about the services, so go to class." How many times did I go to the office and think about my child? How many times did I stay with my child and think about the office? Could I have the ultimate spiritual achievement of being totally *there* in that space and time? Perhaps children are just the ones who can teach us that, for their pasts are short and the future not yet a concern. Watch a small child play, and you will see a totally present being.

As children get older, they become more distracted, more like us. Hank took his family to a Zen Buddhist retreat center for three weeks, a risky adventure with a twelve-year-old kid who loves television and CDs. His eyes glowing with pride, Hank told me, "Rick liked the vacation a lot more than he expected. He loved hanging around the fields, helping to make a compost heap, and, on a lazy morning, taking a book and going 'back to futon.'" The last night, Hank asked Rick what he enjoyed the most. "I was thrilled with his answer," Hank said. "It showed that he really understood what the place was all about. He said, 'What I liked best about being here was being here.'"

Chapter 8

NATURE

Wonder

"Can we go visit 'Nature' today?"

I thought this chapter would be easy to write. So many people I know consider the awe and wonder evoked by the natural world the center of their spiritual lives. For lots of folks, the grandeur and beauty of a mountain peak or an ocean are the origin of their sense of "something more." Long before people have children, they are often touched, their hearts lifted, their urge to pray awakened by a sunset, a flowing creek, a perfect flower. A friend of mine who never talks about religion came home from a vacation on a river in Utah and said simply, "It was God's country."

Surprisingly, however, the parents I interviewed did not spontaneously choose to speak about the natural world. So I had to ask them directly, "How has having children affected your relationship with nature? How have you found ways to share the beauty of nature with your children? Why do you think so few people have mentioned experiences with nature when not specifically asked?"

"When I had children, I could not wait to share with them my reverence for the outdoors," Rob told me. "I remember once riding on a highway with my four-year-old and nearly driving off the road, I was so stunned by the beauty of a setting sun. I tried desperately to get my kid involved in my excitement, but he was playing with a wire toy—I think it was called a Slinky—and he just could not be distracted. Then I realized that for very young kids the whole world is awesome. They don't see the distinction between a really neat toy and a sunset."

"For me," said Hope, "the initial impact of having small children on my relationship with nature was negative. I simply could not get out and be in nature as often as I did before. I was much more limited in the trips I could make, the walks I could take. After one disastrous camping trip with a nursing baby who slept in my sleeping bag and declared the night 'open bar,' we found ourselves spending more time away from nature than in it."

Rob told me about his youthful experiences in the wilderness. "My first wife and I had no children. We spent all our vacations in national forests, far from any other human beings. Sometimes we would be naked for days on end, eating just berries and peanut butter. We would climb mountains and test ourselves against the elements, putting ourselves at risk in order to experience the heightened concentration, the exhilaration. Now that I have children, I would no more do those things than fly to Mars. I feel challenged enough by trying to raise these kids; I hardly need to seek out extra risks."

Parenting ends up teaching us most when we are willing to expand our categories, to see the whole in a tiny part, to throw away the script and be shown a new perspective. I had started off assuming the experience of nature had to be an awesome hike to a majestic site. Parenting brought people many joys, but that was not one of them. When I listened harder, however, I heard many stories of spiritual moments in which parents led their children, and the children led them, to a deeper appreciation of the wonder of creation. Kids see the universe in a grain of sand more easily than we do. They are a lot closer to the ground, and they spend more time getting their hands dirty.

"At first, my kids just kept me inside," Doreen said. "In the end, however, I think they enhanced my love of the natural world. Over the years with small children I learned to enjoy nature in small ways. You don't really need to go so far from home. One fall I took my kids to the park every day, and we gathered autumn leaves. The kids wanted to take them home and look up their names in a book. My five-year-old said, 'If you know the name of something, it can be your friend.' So we borrowed a leaf book from the library. That winter, cooped up in the apartment, we did a lot of art projects with our friends the leaves. If you really pay attention, even one leaf—not to mention a whole bunch—can give you a great deal of joy."

Marc told me this story: "My wife and I made the mistake of taking our kids on a mountain-climbing vacation when the youngest one was too small to really hike. One day, my wife took the older one on a chairlift to climb to a glacier. I stayed back in the valley at the hotel with our three-year-old. We spent the whole day walking around the town looking for tiny wildflowers. By the end of the day we had counted ten different kinds. It wasn't a glacier, but it was miraculous."

Donna, an artist, has chosen to stay at home with her three small children. "I cannot even dream of getting out to someplace beautiful right now. At night, after I get the kids to sleep, I field phone calls from our creditors. Then I go upstairs to my bed to read. My nightstand is piled high with library books. Although I never studied science in college, it is my favorite topic now for evening reading. I read about astronomy, about the mating patterns of elephants, about how physicists believe the world came to be. I feel expansive and inspired. There is more out there in the universe than me and my kids. Much more. The reading sustains me."

For me, one of the unexpected dividends of having children was a new and different connection to the natural world through a most unanticipated dimension—animals. I grew up without pets in my home, and I was ill at ease with (OK, afraid of) animals. To make matters worse, I had allergies. In thirty years, I had mostly steered clear of nonhuman life. Yet I eventually became a mother to pets as well as children. My motive was simple: to relieve the monotony of the days at home with a young child. But I ended up with more than I anticipated.

For our first venture, I selected an animal that was the least threatening to me—a hermit crab. Hermit crabs looked like a lot of fun: my daughter could carry the pet around in a little plastic box; they eat simple household foods and defecate not at all (I still haven't figured out how that is possible). When we went on a vacation, the hermit crab could come along in the box. Also, how sad could we be when a crab dies?

It worked beautifully, and we had some wonderful times watching Hermie race along the driveway, taking him or her (it's hard to tell with a crab) back to the "old country"—the beach. As one might have predicted, Hermie did eventually die. I had assumed that death for a crab meant staying in the shell for longer and longer periods of time until it just never came out anymore. That was the way I would have arranged matters. Unfortunately, nature had other ideas. The death of a hermit crab propels the animal out of the shell where it lies attached by a slender thread to its old home, quite visibly transformed—indeed, quite unmistakably dead. My daughter and I were both surprised by how saddened we were. This taught me that death is never easy, even in the easiest situation. Not a bad lesson for my daughter as well.

Emboldened by the experience, we graduated to gerbils. We bought a male and a female (although we didn't know which was which, the pet store owner assured me we had a fertile couple) and settled down to learn about the beauty of the reproductive process. I had assumed one of the gerbils would grow visibly pregnant, and we could count the days till the blessed event. In fact, it came as a huge surprise. One day when I was alone in the house and talking on the phone, I glanced over to the gerbil cage to see tiny bare gerbils emerging, one after another, from one of the adult gerbils. I felt the holiness of the moment—but only for a short time. My next response was panic. "What do I do?" I asked my friend on the other end of the phone line. "I don't know how to handle this!"

"I don't think you have to *do* anything," she said. "Animals are programmed to handle this kind of thing themselves."

I found it hard to believe that something as enormous as the creation of life could take place without anyone reading any books or involving any professionals. I told my friend I had to get off the phone, and I promptly called the pet store.

"What do I do?" I asked the man who had sold us the gerbils.

"You don't have to *do* anything," he said.

By now, there were seven offspring running about the cage. They eventually settled down to nurse (I finally got straight which adult gerbil was which; the male was the one who still had time to read the newspaper!), and I raced off to pick up my daughter from school. All the way home, I was so excited I thought I would burst out with the news. When she discovered it on reaching home, my daughter was as thrilled as I. Many litters later, my younger daughter was the one who happened by the cage during an unexpected birth experience. It was a highlight of her life.

Pets can expand children's sense of life and its mystery. Sarah obviously had a mother with fewer inhibitions than I concerning animals. "We had lots of animals: rabbits, guinea pigs, tortoises, iguanas, fish, cats, and dogs. At one point we had fifteen animals. There was no argument; whatever we wanted that was living we could have. I was mostly interested in the cats. I was fascinated by their lives outside our home. They would go away for days at a time and come back with their prey. It was a window for me into the jungle, the aspect of life that was not civilized, where living beings killed to eat. I was just enthralled by the animals. The way they moved, the way they smelled. I got to witness their world, which was so different from ours. It humbled me and gave me perspective."

Gardening is also a source of great joy to children and, through them, to parents. Watching the seed become a flower is a miracle, just as it was when the baby was born, and the child is duly impressed. Particularly thrilling are bulbs, planted in the dead of winter as symbols of hope. Just when you have forgotten all about them, one morning your child comes running inside: "Look! Look! There is a flower on our path!"

Sandra shared this story. "When my daughter was six, I told her she could not go to see the movie of *The Secret Garden* until I had read the whole book to her. I figured we would diligently read every night, many chapters, in order to hasten the opportunity to go to the movies. I thought this was a way to cram some good literature down her throat. But I soon discovered she absolutely adored the book and couldn't wait to hear the next chapter. I had no idea what was enchanting her so much or what she was even making of the whole story.

"When we finally went to the movie, she was thrilled. She sat on the edge of her seat for two hours, and I did not see her blink the entire time. When it was over, I asked her what she thought of it. She said she loved the movie but that she wished that they had shown more scenes in which the children were actually digging in the garden and working on it to make it grow. 'The flowers came up so quickly!' she complained. She had understood intuitively that the healing of the depressed children had to do with the process by which they tended the earth and cared for the plants. The movie made it seem like magic. I was amazed by her insight. That afternoon, we went out and got all the paraphernalia to start her own 'secret garden,' which she worked on for many months. The connection between the hard work and the joy in the results was powerful."

Miranda, a single mother, told me a different kind of story about flowers. "One winter my daughter was sick every few weeks. One particular illness lasted a long time. Toward the end of it, I was not feeling all that healthy myself. I called in sick at my office. I didn't want to go out and leave my daughter alone, even to go to the store. After a few days of eating pasta and watching TV, we were both very grouchy. It was a cold, dark winter day. At about two in the afternoon, I realized I was still in my bathrobe. We were sinking. I had to do something. Suddenly, I had an inspiration. I called a florist and ordered a bouquet of spring flowers, a big one. I knew I would be sorry when my credit card bill arrived, but that would be later. Right now, I knew we needed flowers and no one was going to send them to us, so we would just have to send them to ourselves.

"When the doorbell rang and the flowers were delivered, I was sure I had done the right thing. We both sat there for hours just staring at their beauty. They lifted us out of ourselves. A few days later, we were both better."

Shayna shared with me her feelings about the night. For her, the stars were always amazing. "I never really understood what religion was all about until I got out of Los Angeles to the desert. Then I got it. The open, endless space, no segments. When you lie on your back you can see just stars forever. When I learned that what your eye sees as a star is actually light from a glob of gas atoms a million years ago, it made it even more amazing." Shayna agreed with the physicist Richard Feynman that at least in the case of stars, "it does no harm to the mystery to know a little about it."

As a mother, Shayna read her children a book called *Walk When the Moon Is Full.* She decided that if the custom described in the story was good enough for the children in the book, it was good enough for her children. So once a month, on the occasion of the full moon, they would have a nighttime walk to see the stars, to listen to the sounds, and to wonder. The Yiddish poet Aaron Zeitlin warned, "If you look at the stars and yawn . . . then I created you in vain, says God."

Rainbows were always a source of joy to Maureen. When she was cooped up at home with young children, she hung a simple glass crystal in front of her dining room window. Every morning, when the sun came through the crystal, multiple tiny rainbows formed on the opposite wall. If a child touched the crystal and made it move, the rainbows danced. You could see the colors on the dirt-streaked wall, on the milk in the cereal bowl, even on a child's skin if he walked by the path of the light. The magic never ceased.

Ron also found that his children helped him to see the wonder in the natural world. He recalls saving his spare change when his daughter Abby was a toddler to take her to the Philadelphia Zoo. One bright, sunny Sunday they set out on a streetcar and then two buses, paid their admission, and even bought snacks and souvenirs. It was a big deal, and Abby had a fabulous time. But she never once looked at an animal in a cage. What captured her attention were the pigeons who were running loose throughout the zoo. She was simply delighted to chase them all afternoon! At first Ron was disappointed, but eventually he found the experience amusing and even he learned from it. "When I realized that there was a city square right down the street from our apartment filled with pigeons, I was really quite delighted. My daughter taught me that the wonders of nature were actually closer to home than I had realized."

Some families have a "sacred place" outdoors that they enjoy sharing together. Children seem quickly to understand the concept. Pam and her husband and three-year-old loved the spot at the top of the hill near their house. They would often take a picnic there and sit under a tree and relax. They had never officially called it a "sacred place," but one morning, Pam and her daughter were lying in bed and talking. Her daughter was asking, for the millionth time, when they could have another child. Pam explained that the Goddess had not chosen to grace them with that blessing just yet. She suggested that they pray to the Great Mother of All. As Pam opened her mouth to begin the prayer, her daughter put her hand over her mother's mouth and said urgently, "Not here, Mom! We have to say the prayer at the top of the hill!" She knew that the Great Mother would be more accessible there.

During the early days of writing this book, we were snowed in a great deal. At first, all I could think of was how bored the kids would be and how much I wanted to get to work. I spent the first snow days frantically calling people on the phone and digging up videotapes for the kids to watch. When they were settled, I began typing up an interview I had conducted with Eileen, a friend who had moved from the city "back to the land" and raised her sons on a primitive dairy farm, facing the challenges of nature. I was envying her family life on the farm and the obvious gains to the spirit of facing life together in its immediacy, learning self-reliance, exulting in simple pleasures. The irony finally got to me. Here I had an opportunity to live "back to the land" in miniature, and all I could do was try to escape.

A snowstorm or a power failure (or as happened to us later that week, both together) are times when life becomes more primitive than usual. The children respond with utter delight, finding excitement in challenges like shoveling snow or helping to build a fire or walking a mile through the ice to the store for batteries. As adults we are put out by the inconvenience, worried over the mechanics of getting along without our usual equipment, but kids see the adventure in being forced to confront the elements unassisted. If we have the ability to see it from their perspective, we can relax and enjoy what nature has wrought. Forced out of our homes, we can either regret the loss of our comforts or enjoy a long, magnificent walk in the snow.

Some families create this kind of emergency deliberately by going camping. They choose to leave their homes and live in fragile shelters, leave their stoves and cook over a fire they build themselves, leave their television sets and Nintendos and spend the nights watching lizards scamper across the earth. Doug takes his children wilderness camping every summer. He told me why: "You learn more in nature than you do in a mall. I took my three small children hiking into a deep canyon last summer. They were happily swimming in a pool at the bottom when a fierce thunderstorm appeared out of nowhere. We had a four-mile hike back out. The trail rapidly became a stream, and they had to climb up the canyon on all fours, with their socks on their hands. I carried the little one while the other two whined, 'Why did *that* have to happen just when we were having fun?'

"I explained to them that huge rainstorms knock down old trees, which become food and shelter for animals. It really had nothing to do with *their* hike. Nature is much bigger and grander than we are, and learning to respect its beauty and its terror, its generosity and its violence, is a good lesson in humility. I also explained to them that they would have to call up all their reserves of courage and strength to get themselves quickly and safely out of there before it got dark. You don't negotiate with the sunset. It turned out to be a rough passage out, but one that helped my kids understand more about life and about their own resources for meeting its challenges."

Greg loved backpacking and determined that his son, born when Greg was over forty, would feel confident in the wilderness. "I took Max on his first wilderness backpacking trip a month before his fourth birthday. We had matching backpacks and matching red felt hats. We walked three and a half miles to a mountain lake. I wanted him to know what it was like to push himself along a hot, dusty path and then feel the immense joy of peeling off your hiking boots at the end, the cool air on your bare feet. These are life's fundamentals.

"We were relying on each other in the wilderness in a total and intense way that makes a relationship strong. I was completely responsible for his welfare, and, in some sense, he for mine. I explained to him that if I should fall and hit my head (a very unlikely occurrence on that trail), he should stay right by my side and blow his emergency whistle until someone came. I showed him where the food was and how he could keep himself alive until someone rescued us. This is a great deal of responsibility for a little kid, but it helped him conquer fears."

Tina felt that nature was a kind of substitute religion for her parents, and she resented it. Her parents quit their church in anger over politics when Tina was young. They bought a house at the seashore and developed a Sabbath ritual. Every Sunday morning, they drove to the shore. They always took the same walks along the beach. This was their family prayer life. Her mother would point to the sunset and say, defiantly, "That's *my* idea of God. When things get too much for me back home, I think about this spot and everything gets into perspective again." Tina loved their house at the shore, but she always felt her parents were "holding out on her," that there was something more they were keeping from her.

When she became an adult, Tina came to believe that for her, it was faith in God that ultimately put everything in her life in perspective. She joined a church and also continued to love sunsets. When she had children, she did not want them to think they had to choose between church and nature. So she found a summer family camp that was run by the national headquarters of her church. There, on the shores of a beautiful lake, the family sat on the ground and heard Bible stories, played games, discussed issues, and visited the "Green Chapel" morning and evening for group prayers, more often for individual meditation.

Paula was concerned that Judaism and her son did not seem to "click." Paula had always loved services: the prayers, the songs, the Torah stories. But she had to admit that seeing it from her son Dan's perspective, it *was* an awful lot of words. "You know that prayer in the liturgy," she asked me, "the one that says, 'If our mouths were as full of words as the ocean, we could not praise one-thousandth of your goodness'? It seems that doesn't keep us from trying!"

Paula noticed that Dan shut down completely during services but really came alive when he was studying birds in science class or walking through a creek on a Cub Scout outing. It was not until Dan was eight that Paula realized that long before that thick prayer book was written, Judaism was a religion of the earth. There were still many paths back. That fall, Paula and her husband built a sukkah, an outdoor dwelling with leafy branches for a roof, and the first night of the festival of Sukkot, at the full moon, the whole family slept in the sukkah. The next morning, as they awoke to birds singing instead of the clock radio, Dan looked up from his sleeping bag blissfully. The pieces of his world were beginning to come together.

For some families, their love of nature goes beyond wonder and appreciation. Their concern for the environment results in specific practices designed to respect and honor the natural world. The way in which we eat can be a spiritual path. Marla's family is involved with no organized faith, but they have a "religion" of their own: vegetarianism based on a moral concern for animals. Long before their children were born, Marla and her husband committed themselves to a strict vegetarian diet. In addition, they decided to conserve natural resources by never using disposable materials for eating in their home.

Marla's children were teenagers when she told me about the surprising consequences of their practices. "Neither of my children have ever eaten an animal in their lives. Nor have we ever had paper plates or plastic at our family table. We were prepared to be flexible with them if necessary, but our children totally embraced our practice and have never challenged it. Although we did not give them a religious faith, we did give them this. It provided a kind of identity for our family. I think it taught them that they could be different from others and that was OK. It taught them that you have a choice about what you do, that what you do matters, that you can make ethical commitments in your daily life, and that you can live by a principle—in this case, respect for animals and the natural world. I now see that the way we eat is our spiritual practice as a family."

The summer I was finishing this book, I fasted for twenty-six hours, alone on a mountain ridge in California. I spent one sunny day building a lean-to out of a tarp and one majestic, windswept night amid endless snow and countless stars. When I got back, people asked me how my solo adventure compared to parenting. After all, I was writing a book about the spiritual experience of parenting and had just had a very different kind of spiritual experience. How were they different, how were they the same?

First, the differences. While both parenting and surviving outdoors alone are difficult, parenting (just for the record) is much *more* difficult. It is also noisier, messier, more complicated, takes much longer, and requires more equipment.

On the other hand, although parenting and solo camping are quite unlike one another, what makes them both spiritual is precisely the same thing. It is the mystery.

The more I looked out at the view from my site, across the mountains to Lake Tahoe in the distance, the less I knew it, the more enigmatic, magical, mystical, and unfathomable it seemed. The more I know my children, the deeper and longer our relationship becomes, the less I feel I really understand about them, the more I come to honor the ultimately ineffable forces that go into creating their separate selves. Both the wilderness and my children, in different ways, connect me with the enigma of life, remind me of how little I can finally account for or understand. But I can certainly appreciate the blessing of meeting them (my children) and seeing it (Lake Tahoe) in my lifetime.

The Orthodox Jewish thinker Samson Raphael Hirsch, as an old man, insisted on traveling from his home in Germany to Switzerland. When asked why, he explained that soon he would be standing before his Maker. "I will be held answerable to many questions. But what will I say when I am asked, 'Shimshon, did you see my Alps?'"

Saint Augustine said, "Men go abroad to wonder at the height of mountains . . . and they pass by themselves without wondering."

A young mother I know called me a few days after her daughter was born. She was sleep deprived and incoherent, but among her ecstatic ramblings I remember one bold declaration: "She's more beautiful than Yosemite National Park!" When parents meet their Maker, if they have had their eyes open and been willing to be surprised, they can surely affirm they have seen God's wonders.

PART 3

Evening

DINNERTIME

Thankfulness

"We have been given so much—we pray for a grateful heart."

Dinnertime. From the western window, a beautiful red haze illuminates the dining room. The children, clean and scrubbed, dressed in their finest, are lined up in front of their seats, ready to sing grace. A table is set, a royal banquet, and the food is all ready, simmering warm on the stove. The answering machine is on, ready to intercept phone calls. TVs and CDs are silenced. Candles are lit, wine poured. There is peace in the home, peace in the hearts, and the family is ready for the moment when once again they will acknowledge their gratitude at the end of the day. Everyone is eager to break bread together, nourish body and soul, and in the words of the psalm, "taste and see that the Lord is good."

As my kids would say: "NOT!" This dream is certainly not our family reality. Some families eat dinner one at a time, an arrangement made possible by frozen foods and microwave ovens. Others eat together but in a rush, unaware that something special is going on. In our house, we all try to consume food at the same table at more or less the same time while speaking a few reasonable words to one another. Some nights we achieve a great deal more; some nights less.

From my studies of religion, I know that sharing food is potent, laden with meaning. After the Temple in Jerusalem was destroyed, Jews began to treat their own family dinner table as the altar, their meal as the sacred occasion at which they met God. The salting of meat reminds us of the preparation of the sacrifice. In Christianity, the breaking and sharing of bread is the central rite. According to the Gospel of Luke, when Jesus returned from the dead and sat among his disciples he did not immediately offer great metaphysical truths. In fact, his first interest was rather basic. "Does anyone have anything to eat?" he asked. To become companions literally means to share bread together. And the Hindu master Vivekananda said, "First bread, and then religion."

Nina, the Amish woman who threw her clothes out the train window as she left her community, knows about the power of eating. She still lovingly returns to her home to visit family and friends who lovingly welcome her. When it is time to eat, however, a separate table must be set for Nina. According to the time-honored laws of shunning passed down through the generations in an oral tradition, Amish people may not dine with those who have been excommunicated. The tradition, although more rigid and exclusive than many of us would like, underscores how intimate an act it is to share a meal.

For some families, transforming eating into an occasion for spiritual sustenance comes naturally. When I was speaking in a small town in Minnesota, I met the wife of an Episcopal priest who told me about her family ritual. Every night she lights candles and puts church music on the stereo. Then she and her husband sit down quietly and graciously at opposite ends of the table. Having set the tone, they are then joined by the children.

One woman I spoke to grew up in a tightly knit community organized around a church. It was the custom among families in that church to read the Bible together after dinner. Everyone knew the rules. You would not think of calling someone between 7:00 and 7:30 in the evening. That time was claimed for the family, the Bible, and the Lord.

But few of us live in communities with established norms around family dinners; most of us make it up as we go along. Trish recalls that in her interethnic, somewhat eccentric childhood home, there was no formal talk of religion. But each night at dinner the family would hold hands and say, "Bon appetit," in as many languages as the people at the table knew. On a good night, with several guests, the litany would take quite a while. Once completed, people felt connected, ready to share their food and themselves.

Some families begin their ritual life when their children come home from nursery school with prayers they have learned. For example, Lee told me, "Our daughter said a prayer at nursery school before snack: 'Isn't it nice to eat with friends?' She liked it so much she insisted on doing it at home. So we held hands and said, 'Isn't it nice to eat with family!' We started off saying it really fast and kind of embarrassed, but the baby would look up and beam. When our daughter switched nursery schools, we switched prayers. Now we said, 'God is great, God is good, let us thank God for our food.' My husband and I would look at each other and think, 'What are two atheists doing praying nightly?' But we wanted some small way to celebrate our lives. By now, we all look forward to our evening prayer. We even light a candle, which has an amazingly calming effect. Everyone makes eye contact, and we slow down internally. It is a time of connection, of touching base."

Still, you are wondering, who can gather the whole family for a home-cooked dinner every night of the week? For many families, including my own, there is a middle ground: one night a week is special. One night a week, with or without community support, the family claims a holy time for themselves. Said Lyn, "My dad was a doctor and he was rarely home for dinner. But Friday night was different. Our family revolved around Friday night. When I was old enough to talk, my first questions were: Is it Friday yet? How much longer till Friday? That was how I began the process of conceptualizing time. Friday night we all ate dinner together and performed some of the rituals of the Sabbath. It was the scaffolding of our family, the centerpiece of the family life."

Fred spent his childhood in a chaotic, emotionally confused home. He explained, "We never ate together, except by chance. I determined that when I had children it would be different. I wanted to give my son the sense of rhythm that I had missed so much. At first, I thought we would have a ritual: an orderly breakfast and dinner at the same time each morning and night. But as the years passed, life became more complicated. We began our days at different times. The kids had different activities in the afternoons. The one thing we held on to was Sunday dinner."

Many people have powerful memories of special dinners. Karen recalls that as a little child it was her job to pick flowers and put them on the table before Sunday dinner. For Mark, the special family time was Saturday night. The rest of the week was variable, but Saturday night was "sacred." The family always enjoyed steak, French-fried onion rings, string beans, popcorn, and each other. Regular Friday night dinners punctuated Vicki's childhood. The family would light candles and name all the relatives who had died or were far away. When she thinks back to her childhood, the memory of all those dinners, each alike in their ritual sameness, merge together into a warm glow.

Violet remembers Sunday nights at her Aunt Jane's. "It was solid and safe, the place to be. It was the right thing to be doing." In Violet's Bible is the handwritten copy of the prayer her family has said for three generations at the Sunday dinner table. She knows it by heart. Divorced now, without children at home, on Sunday nights Violet makes herself a nicer than usual dinner, sets the table for one, and reads the prayer aloud to herself.

Breaking bread together is a classic opportunity to express gratitude. Christians say grace before a meal and Jews after it is over. Muslims begin a meal with the same words they use to begin any task, "In the name of God, the all-Merciful, the Compassionate," and the more observant will end the meal with the verse that follows that one in the Koran, "Praise to God, the Lord of all the worlds." When I spent some time among Zen Buddhists, I loved their simple grace before meals, which included these words:

> *Innumerable labors brought*
> *us this food.*
> *The work of many people*
> *and the suffering of other forms*
> *of life.*

The volumes of mealtime prayers could be succinctly summarized: thank you. Deep in our primitive selves, we are all afraid of starving to death alone. When we sit down with others to eat, the ancient wisdom tells us to notice and be glad.

Cathy told me that when it comes to spiritual life, gratitude is her path. "When I was a young mother, before I knew anything about prayer or meditation, my 'spiritual practice' was photography. I was always grabbing the camera and trying to capture moments. When the kids were all dressed up and their shoes shined or when one child had a look of complete joy on her face, I would run for the camera. I think of those photos now as my blessings, uttered before I knew about blessings or how to say them. They were an effort to freeze time and say, This is worthy of being acknowledged. Thank you. I didn't yet have a sense of whom or what I was thanking."

Sometimes when I talked to people about their childhood, they would say that their parents had no explicit religious interests. Then they would add, "But deep inside, my mother was a very religious person." When I tried to probe what that meant, I got a sense it had something to do with the person's attitude toward life, a kind of humility. One woman recalled, "My mother never sat down and talked to me about what she believed. I don't recall anything like that ever happening. But she had a lot of phrases that she always used in her conversation. She would say, 'We're going to a party Sunday, if God wills it.' I don't think she believed that literally (why would God, if He existed, *not* want us to go to the party?), but it was an expression of an attitude. She taught me never to take anything for granted, to see it all as a gift."

Parents experience gratitude as a result of their children; they also try to teach their children gratitude. How does one teach children to feel grateful, or at least to say "thank you"? "It is easy," says Miss Manners. "You tell them once when they are young. Then you repeat it five hundred thousand times a year until they turn eighteen."

Some parents teach their children gratitude through the act of noticing, through saying a blessing or a prayer. "To eat something without saying a blessing is like stealing," Ken was taught. Or as Alice Walker put it, "I think it pisses God off if you walk by the color purple in a field somewhere and don't notice." As a father, Ken would take walks with his daughter and whenever they saw something beautiful Ken would say a blessing. "Now my daughter looks for things to bless too."

Children seem to take quickly to the idea of blessings. In Jewish traditions, it is written that a person should say a minimum of one hundred blessings a day. Children understand. One young girl I interviewed told me that her mother taught her to say a blessing before she ate anything at all. She confided, "My mother doesn't know this, but when I feed my cat I always say a blessing for him before he eats. It's only fair."

Jews recite the *shehechianu* blessing whenever something is done for the first time, or for the first time in a season or year. The blessing thanks God for "keeping us alive, sustaining us, and enabling us to be here to experience this moment." Jackie was taught to say this blessing the first time in a season she ate a particular fruit or vegetable. It was one of the few surviving rituals in her family's Judaism. She has continued the custom, adding the first time they go swimming in the ocean each summer. To Jackie's great delight, the first time her daughter whistled, out came the blessing from her daughter's mouth! And Jackie repeated it, for it was the first time her daughter had said *shehechianu* on her own—certainly an occasion for blessing.

Batya was overwhelmed with two small children and a part-time baby-sitter "who also seemed to need a lot of care." One Friday, Batya announced to her husband that she was going AWOL. She got into the car, drove to the seashore, and went for a long walk alone by the beach. Then she entered a restaurant and ordered a split of champagne and a whole lobster—a great way to "act out" for Batya, who had always observed the Jewish laws concerning unclean animals. When she put the first fork full of lobster in her mouth, Batya found herself uttering the *shehechianu* blessing. It was, after all, the first time she had ever eaten this food! The system from which she was fleeing had overtaken her. Monday morning, Batya was back at her post.

Gratitude is also about thanking one another. Ironically, the people in our lives we are least likely to thank and appreciate are the people closest to us.

In Jewish homes, each Friday night the husband traditionally reads to his wife the passage from Proverbs about "the woman of valor." While often dismissed as pedestal polishing, this simple act is instructive. Would it be so terrible if we all told our spouses once a week what we appreciated about them? Or our children? In some homes, families go around the table each evening and share "something new and good today." Thanking is a way of life; praise is a habit. For many families, ritual is one way to create a culture of appreciation.

Simply dressing up for an occasion is a sign of respect. What a revelation to realize we can do that for our own families! Shoshana Silberman, a Jewish educator, writes that she always prepared a festive Sabbath dinner for her family, whether or not guests were invited. One of her children said to her, "You must think we kids are pretty important if you put out your best silver just for us."

For people who have a dinner routine, daily or weekly or less frequently, the routine is more important than the food. Marvin's family observes Friday night dinner in a special way. "Shabbat dinner is important because we always do it. We always have the same food. We always discuss whether to sing the long or the short blessing over the wine. We always decide on the short one. It's a sure thing."

Ritual adds majesty to the ordinary act of eating a meal. Part of the traditional Jewish dinner is the ritual washing of the hands with a prescribed three rinses and a special cup. This ritual recalls the hand washing of the priests before they partook of the sacrificial meal in the Temple in Jerusalem. The family dinner table symbolizes the altar. This hand washing is not about physical cleaning. It is about intention.

Ellen began observing a ritual hand washing with her children before dinner when they were quite young, although she was not sure they would understand what it was all about. After they washed and said the blessing, her four-year-old looked up with her face beaming and said, "I feel even cleaner than if I washed my hair!" Said Ellen, "I realized that when it came to ritual, my daughter really got it!"

This doesn't mean parents always find it easy to engage children in their agenda for the dinner celebration. One mother explained, "It was always really important for me that Friday dinner be an oasis in time, a special chance at living on a higher, holier level than the rest of the week. When my kids were little, I wanted this to happen so much that I worked and worried all day Friday to have it go off in a flawless way. I'd even check the silverware to make sure the pieces were all lined up, something I never did during the week. Of course, when it came time to gather at the table, the kids would fight terribly—no worse than they fought the rest of the week, but it would hurt more. It was usually an enormous disappointment; I would often end up in tears.

"But we just kept at it, and eventually they learned and I learned. They learned that at least half the time they could be little princes in a royal court for ten minutes, and something rather beautiful would happen. And I learned that at least half the time I just couldn't control life enough to have it my way, and I'd have to let go of my fantasy and enjoy whatever happened."

Another mother came up with a solution that worked for her. "When my kids were little, they resisted our special Sunday dinner, perhaps just because they sensed it was so important to me and they needed a way to rebel, to separate from me. When Sunday night came, they would be grouchy rather than pleasant. I decided to bribe them by having better food on Sunday nights, desserts that weren't offered the rest of the week.

It worked! It gave them a focus when they were young. As they got older, the other aspects began to make sense to them."

John had a different approach. "Our kids learned religion by acting. When our children were already in elementary school, my wife and I decided to begin observing the Sabbath with a Friday night ritual dinner. At first it felt awkward; the kids were not at all sure they wanted to be part of this. So we started inviting over other families, people who knew even less than we did about the rituals. Now my kids became the show-offs—acting 'as if' all this were natural and helpfully explaining everything to the guests. I've heard people say, 'Fake it till you make it.' It works. Pretty soon, the ritual was natural for us. Even when there was no audience, the kids performed the script and felt good about it. In the beginning, we needed the audience to make us less embarrassed in front of each other."

Families without a weekly dinner ritual still have special dinners, such as holidays when, as the poet Linda Pastan wrote about the Passover seder, we "set our table with metaphor." Some families enjoy special dinners around their birthdays, their ancestors' birthdays, or their pets' birthdays. Others have holidays unique to their own family, such as the Jewish clan I know who celebrate "What's-a-Jew-to-Do-Day" (otherwise known as December 25).

Dinnertime is often the moment when people gather and note whatever special event has occurred within the family. One mother told me, "When my daughter got her period for the first time, she was embarrassed and didn't want it discussed. But we bought some flowers and put them at her place at the table. Then we lit candles and had a nicer than usual dinner that night. Not a word was uttered. It was our way of saying it was a special night for all of us."

Thanksgiving dinner is, of course, the premier example of this combination of food, family, and gratitude. One mother I met writes notes to each family member on Thanksgiving, detailing all that she is thankful for about that person and her relationship with them. A Jewish family I know, echoing the custom of hiding a piece of matzah that enchants children at seders, instituted the custom of hiding the wishbone of the turkey. The popularity of Thanksgiving is attributable to its simplicity. There is no esoteric ritual or complicated liturgy. You count your blessings and enjoy your food. Feasting together makes us feel safe.

I have been moved by the way in which ritual behavior is alive and well in families. All over America, people bake birthday cakes, decorate them, light candles, make wishes, blow out candles. This isn't in any religious tome. Someone made the whole thing up to punctuate the birthday meal, to make it special. In the American Jewish community, there is a custom that builds on the birthday-candle routine. As a rabbi, I held one opinion of this ritual. As a student of the spiritual lives of families, I have come to a very different judgment.

This particular custom does not take place in the synagogue, where thirteen-year-olds traditionally mark their coming of age by being called to the Torah for the first time. In fact, it has nothing to do with the Torah. It occurs at the festive meal that follows the service. The child calls up thirteen relatives or friends to light the candles on the birthday cake. Since it is usually Saturday afternoon and still the Sabbath, the candle lighting is actually contrary to Jewish law. This ritual of unknown origins (rumor attributes it to a caterer on Long Island in the 1950s) is so popular and so meaningful to some Jews that it feels as emotionally important as the Torah service.

As a rabbi, I disapproved of the whole matter. I thought family and friends should be honored as part of the service in the synagogue, not in a "meaningless" American custom of lighting candles on a cake. But looking at it from the point of view of American Jews, the ritual makes all kinds of sense. The meal is an important time of sharing and celebrating—it should have a ritual component. Further, the thirteen-year-old wants to honor those people who are most important in his or her life. They may include, among others, children who are too young to participate in a long, boring service (and it is not only the very young who have this problem!), non-Jewish friends and relatives who often will not be allowed a part in the synagogue proceedings, an elderly grandmother who will not join in the service because she still believes it is "really" for men. But everyone can light a candle. And everyone does! Families wanted to be sure all the treasured friends and family got into the act. They were right to take things into their own hands.

Sometimes, gratitude is evoked in the most unlikely ways—not at a life-cycle passage but on an ordinary, even difficult day.

Susan was raised in a halfhearted Christian home with no observance of religion except once or twice a year. As an adult she joined a church, but "the classes were too intellectual and the spiritual programs too outer space." As she put it, "I just didn't get it. I couldn't find my place in the religious scene. I also did a lot of searching in the psychological sphere: est, twelve steps, therapy. Why wasn't I happier? Why did I keep switching jobs? Why did I overeat?

"Later, I had my perfect family—one boy, one girl, a house in the suburbs, a husband who came home for dinner at six. I kept up with the church but only for the sake of the children. Spirituality was a nonissue for me. My third child was unplanned. When he was born physically and mentally handicapped, I crashed. I sank into a deep depression. Pulling myself out, I started to walk through my life again. I would take Josh to the supermarket, and well-meaning strangers would come up to me and say, 'God knew what he was doing in giving you this special child.' I found that so unacceptable, I wanted to throw a can of beans at them.

"Josh is now three. Sometimes when it is dinnertime and I'm too tired to get the food on the table, I think I'm finally going to give up. Just then, Josh toddles into the kitchen all hugs and smiles. What was it I was looking for in spirituality? I can't remember. There's nothing to search for—it's all right here. I have everything I ever wanted in life, everything that life could offer, right here in this moment of pure love. *In this moment.* I am flooded with blessing, awash in gratitude. I know it doesn't make any sense. Why am I learning gratitude from the child who poses the most problems for me? He keeps reminding me what a gift life is. I don't know why. I can only tell you that is what happened."

Gratitude is not about perfection but about noticing how blessed we are. Saying thanks is not always about feeling thankful. Sometimes it is a way of creating an inner shift. One of my students said, "When you get older, joy becomes a decision, celebration a conscious choice." Richard told me about his childhood as a very poor farm boy. The family would sit at the table, their heads bowed, and his mother would say, "This food may not be what we want, and it may not be how much we want, but we still should give thanks for it being here." Then they would dig in to their meal of potatoes or cabbage. Dorothy, also from a poor family, told me that her father never failed to say grace. Together, they would pray, "May we see thy goodness in our daily bread."

One woman reported with shame about a time when she realized how much her young son needed to learn. It occurred to Rose that it would be nice to bring a turkey to a homeless shelter on Thanksgiving Day. She told her five-year-old about the idea. He replied quickly, with a bright look on his face, "We don't need to do that! If those people have to live in a shelter, then they don't have anything to be thankful for. So they don't need to celebrate Thanksgiving!"

"I was devastated by that remark," Rose confessed. "I realized that the kid was smart but that he lacked compassion. He was more interested in the clever retort than in helping people. How glad I was that I had decided to do this Thanksgiving turkey project! It was not a minute too soon!"

As I thought about this story, I realized how Rose's little boy had unwittingly provided the opening for a teaching about what gratitude is all about. Because the truth is, people in shelters *do* celebrate Thanksgiving, as do people in cancer wings of hospitals and all kinds of other difficult circumstances. When Seth and I visited the United States Holocaust Memorial Museum in Washington, D.C., we were both transfixed by a particular survivor speaking to us on an oral history video. We were so moved we watched the whole video through so we could hear his words a second time. The old man, recalling his time in Auschwitz fifty years ago, tells about hearing the man next to him in the barracks praising God. "I could not believe it! I asked him, 'Why would you thank God in this hell? What in the world are you thanking God *for?*' Do you know what that man told me? He said, 'I am thanking God that I was not created like the murderers around me.'"

Those of us who eat dinner in our homes with our families sometimes find it easy to catalog our complaints. But people in the most difficult straits are moved to give thanks for that which is good in their lives. Whether our dinner is simple or elaborate, peaceful or chaotic, daily or weekly, how much more should we acknowledge and bless whatever forces there are that we have been kept alive, sustained, and enabled to be here to experience this moment!

Chapter 10

WATCHING THE NEWS

Justice

"I wanted the war and the chicken pox to be over."

We create a sanctuary of love and connection and call it home. Then we turn on the television set to watch the evening news. Before long, our children are watching too, and whatever illusions we had are shattered. It is just as well, for religion is not a private hobby. We can discover religious experience in the family, but religion ultimately propels us out of the home to where human beings are most in need. We create a safe and loving home in order to leave it. And it is often our children who push us out the door.

Edith, who lives in a suburb of Philadelphia, decided to take her kids for a treat to the center of the city to see the Liberty Bell and Independence Hall. While walking from one monument to the next, her twelve-year-old daughter Joan saw for the first time homeless people lying on the sidewalk. The outing was to culminate with ice cream at a fancy restaurant. But Joan couldn't eat. What was supposed to have been an enjoyable outing to instill pride in our country had turned out to be an upsetting day, leaving Joan with a lump in her throat.

Edith concluded that she should take her children to Philadelphia much more often and that whenever they went they needed to pack bag lunches to distribute to people who were hungry. So they did. A few months later, Joan said, "Mom, it's getting cold and some of the homeless people aren't wearing shoes." So the next time, they brought four pairs of her dad's discarded shoes.

Our children's sense of justice embarrasses us with our own complacency. Children's insights are not merely aesthetic or even moral. An unjust society will be a terrible place for them to live, an unworthy legacy from parents to children. Also, becoming parents often makes us feel more powerfully our connection to other parents. Stan recalls, "The morning after my first child was born I was driving through North Philadelphia to the hospital. On a street corner I saw a mother standing there with her child, a woman who was clearly struggling to keep her child in food and clothes. I felt so close to this woman whom I had never seen before. We shared this incredible bond, knew the same secret. How could I not care about her welfare or that of her child?"

In America today, there is a terrible shortage of safe blood. Every parent knows that if his child needed it, he would drain the blood from his veins every morning and evening. But there are children who need blood right now. Ann Landers once printed a letter about a mother who gave blood to the American Red Cross every year on the birthdays of her children. God had given her gifts—living, healthy children. This was her birthday present back.

What if every parent in America volunteered to give blood every year on each of the birthdays of their children? Giving a pint of blood twice a year is only a tiny beginning, but children too are only tiny beginnings. If there is one thing we have learned from the spiritual journey of parenthood, it is to treasure even that which is small and not yet finished.

So we do small acts, and our children see them and remember. Kathy grew up in the mountains of Tennessee in a devout Protestant home. She remembers knowing at an early age that her parents tithed their income, following the biblical mandate to give 10 percent of what they earned to the church. In turn, she was required to tithe her allowance, and she did so with pride. Rela grew up in the South Bronx in a Jewish family with little money. A *pushke* (a small metal box) was hung on the wall to collect their contributions—a penny at a time—for the poor Jews in Palestine. It was a bit of folk superstition that no one actually believed anymore, but if a child was sick or a big exam was coming up, putting a penny in the box was said to help. If Rela got ten cents for Chanukah, her mother told her to put one of them in the box: "It isn't really yours until you give some of it away." Rela remembers a night when there was no money, just potatoes in the house, and someone suggested opening the full *pushke* and borrowing against their accumulated donations to buy themselves food. But her parents said, "Absolutely not!" and Rela never forgot how rich that made her feel.

As an adult with many more resources than her parents, Rela included the *pushke* and its equivalent in every aspect of her children's lives. Once they were vacationing in Quebec and stopped at a gas station because they were hopelessly lost. A Catholic priest heard them asking questions and offered to guide them to their destination. After he did so, he drove away before they could thank him. Rela immediately decided that at the next church they saw they would make a charitable contribution in honor of the priest. When the family entered the church and explained their mission, they were told to put the money in a box (a *pushke!*) for Saint Anthony, the patron saint of the lost. The kids never forgot that adventure nor the point behind it: "You give back."

Marjorie can recall as a child driving late at night with her grandmother around their small town. The pair would stop at the homes of people in the church whom Grandmother knew were in need of some extra money. Marjorie's job was to jump out of the car and deposit a small, unmarked envelope filled with cash on the person's doorstep.

John's son came home from Sunday school enchanted by the idea that the Israelites in the Bible would leave the corners of their fields unharvested so that the poor could come and gather food. Living in New York City, Mitchell had no fields to harvest or to leave unharvested, but his father suggested that the modern-day equivalent of the corners would be spare change. Every time Mitchell spent money, he would save the "extra," the change, in a special box. When he had enough, he would bring it to Sunday school and hand it over to the church's charity fund.

Many parents encourage their own children's giving. Susan set up a "matching-grants program" through which she offers to match any amount her son gives to a charitable cause with an equal amount of her own money.

Some parents try to avoid the excesses of materialism that accompany Christmas (and now Chanukah as well) by turning the matter inside out. Said Evan, "Christmas is supposed to be about giving, so we focus on our giving as a family. In December, we are deluged by end-of-the-tax-year requests from all the nonprofit groups we support. We keep them in a huge carton. Each night during the Christmas holiday season we sit around the fire and read the letters and brochures, discussing with the children the problems these various organizations seek to address. Then we plan what percent of our giving should go to each group."

Some families make contributions to causes instead of giving gifts, both to their own children and to others. Grace told me that she got tired of buying yet another toy for yet another privileged child's birthday party. One day she just decided, "No more!" Now she routinely sends her child to the party with a note that a contribution to the school scholarship fund has been made in the birthday child's honor. While she had expected some flak, she reported that children were actually pleased by the thought that their birthday had contributed in some small way to others.

Kids have an innate sense of justice. Despite their natural egoism, they want to help others. We can confirm and strengthen their compassion when we give children the opportunities to respond to injustice and affirm the good feelings those responses create.

Around the time of his fifth birthday, Della's son Arthur was terribly worried about hungry people. He came up with the idea of what he called a "poor party." He wanted written on the birthday invitations that everyone was to bring one can of food for poor people. He explained that with the cans he would set up a free store for poor people in his basement. Della was eager not to squash his dreams, so she agreed to the idea about the invitation. She gently explained that it was unlikely many poor people would find their way to his basement but that together they could deliver all the cans to a shelter. And they did.

My daughter, fresh from her reading of Laura Ingalls Wilder's *Little House* series, wondered why the homeless people in our city couldn't go out to the country, build small cabins, and farm the land like Laura and her family did. We tried not to mock her idealism and naïveté, and to our own surprise discovered that there actually *was* a small homesteader movement that took homeless men from New York City and taught them to farm in the far north of New York state. As a family, we made the six-hour drive to check out this farm. Satisfied with the work being done, our daughter subsequently enjoyed supporting this good cause and convinced her Hebrew school class to support it as well. It was, after all, her idea.

Eileen watched as her daughter June struggled with problems of her own and eventually created out of her troubles a project to help others. June began to have serious bouts of asthma when she was nine. By the time she was twelve, she had spent hundreds of hours in doctors' offices and not a few nights in hospitals. Because her parents were educated and had money, they were able to get her the care she needed. Eileen was always bracing herself for the question from June, "Why me? None of my friends have to miss every camping trip because of asthma. None of my friends spent the night before the first day of school in the hospital. Why?" But June never asked.

When she was about twelve, June learned to her dismay that in the inner cities of this country asthma is the leading cause of death in children her age. Most of these deaths were avoidable, if children and their parents knew what she and her parents knew about the disease and its management. So June decided to write a book about what it was like to be a kid with asthma—both the emotional experience and the tactics she had learned to keep herself as safe as possible.

June hoped the book would be useful to children with asthma, particularly those who did not have the resources of her own family. She realized that it would be helpful to have a coauthor, someone who could report on the experience of having severe asthma as a child *without* educated parents, health insurance, and the like. The obvious candidate presented herself at the door the next day! June's grandmother, who had emigrated from Europe as a young child, had grown up in the slums of New York, struggling almost alone with a case of asthma as debilitating as her granddaughter's. The grandmother's parents knew neither the language nor the system and barely understood their daughter's health problems. So granddaughter and grandmother decided to write the book together.

We need to make giving to others part of everyday life. Gretchen had a seemingly trivial but novel approach. Whenever she thought of it, she would give her children a handful of coins and let them go up and down the streets plugging expired meters. It was a way to give a little anonymous gift to a stranger. Another father also enjoyed anonymous giving on a very small scale. Periodically, when he went through a tollbooth he would pay double and tell the guard to let the next person go through "on the house."

While these rituals are more fun than profound, they dramatize, on a child's level, the use of one's resources to benefit others.

What does all this have to do with a serious response to the injustice of the world? It takes more than distributing sandwiches, giving blood, plugging meters, or sending checks to solve our world's problems. But small practices may develop a momentum of their own. Edith, after many trips to the city with her children, realized that it was not enough to bring lunches and shoes. Her daughter's reaction to the birthplace of the nation has since led Edith to join an interfaith action group that is fighting for better housing in the city. Our spirituality as parents can ultimately lead us, each in our own way—as teachers, writers, lawyers, nurses, businesspeople, volunteers—to address the broad systemic problems that mar the life of our society with avoidable injustice.

Kim grew up in Miami among poor Chinese immigrants. "My father did not speak to me about injustice or ethics; he just lived it. We had a tiny apartment, but the living room was always filled with folding beds. At any given time, there would always be two or three new arrivals working at restaurants all day and evening and camping out in our house at night. That is the way life was. So now, in our home, my partner and I do the same. We have had refugees from Vietnam, from Cambodia. We have had people with AIDS and people about to be deported. My three-year-old does not get lectures, she gets houseguests.

"I also want to teach my daughter that one fights injustices against oneself. I am gay and also Chinese. I sit on the board of an organization that champions the rights of Chinese-Americans and also one for gay and lesbian civil rights. I take my daughter to all the board meetings. She plays in a corner, but I am hoping that as the years go on, she will get the idea that you have to go out and work to defend yourself and your concerns. She is not Chinese, and she very well may not be gay, but she will have her own issues, and my partner and I want her to learn to be a strong spokesperson for them."

Some rare people make fighting injustice a part of their own lives and their children's from the first day to the last. When someone asked fifteen-year-old Ian how he felt seeing his mother Martha taken to jail for an antinuclear protest she had organized, he answered proudly, "My mom has been in jail hundreds of times!" I interviewed Martha at a time when I was writing the chapter on death and limits. I asked her how she answered her children's questions. She responded by talking about her life as a social activist.

Martha raised her children in a small, alternative community linked by commitments to social justice rather than to any historic religious tradition. The group lived together in a series of communally owned homes over a period of years. The adults in these homes all worked for social change both at their jobs and in their spare time. "We often had refugees from oppression sheltered in our community. My kids learned about suffering and death very early. They heard the most horrible stories at the dinner table. The good part was that they didn't come upon these issues later in life as philosophical problems. They can't tell you the day they first realized life is unfair. They don't remember a time when they *didn't* know that the world is filled with atrocities and injustice. They never asked why. They always knew that was a nonstarter. The question was, When do we start organizing?"

For most people, however, Martha's path is not their own, especially not after they have children. There is no denying that parenthood changes the way we understand these issues. One moonless December night twelve years ago, I lay in a hospital bed, a symphony of exaltation playing in my brain. The most perfect, the most beautiful, the most miraculous of creatures, my firstborn child—not even one day old—lay just down the hall and would soon be brought to my bedside. In a moment, we would be nursing together.

Suddenly, a nurse appeared in the doorway. "There is something wrong with your child. We are taking her down to the intensive care unit." The symphony screeched to a halt. Suffering had taken on a whole new dimension—it was my baby's suffering now, more frightening to me than my own. I lay there, perhaps three minutes, perhaps three hours.

The nurse reappeared. "I'm terribly sorry. I confused the charts. Your child is fine. I'm bringing her right in." The symphony did not begin again. Instead, I listened as the nurse walked down the hall to some unknown woman for whom the news was actually meant. I felt a kinship for her, a deep connection that knew nothing of race or religion and made those categories seem trivial and mean. I would do anything to help her.

At the same time, there was a contrary truth: all I really cared about now was my milk coming in for my baby. I had never felt so filled to the brim with love that flowed outward toward the whole world. Yet I had also never felt so protective of my own self and my boundaries, so ungenerous toward anything that would stand in the way of my child's welfare. At the same time that I was becoming more compassionate, I was also gaining a good excuse for being more selfish.

Before I had children, I had preached about justice. I had said the sort of things liberal religious people usually say, like "The ideal of justice is based on the assumption that human beings are intrinsically equal. . . . Injustice enters through the door of biased treatment." As a religious idealist, I believed the babies in that nursery were of equal (and infinite) value, and it was no matter if one was sick or another. But now I was a mother. As a mother, my baby mattered a whole lot more. Would I rather my baby were well and *three* of the others in the nursery be sick? You bet! (I later interviewed a devout Quaker who confessed to me that she was indeed an orthodox pacifist, except in one situation: if someone was threatening the lives of her children.) Fighting injustice is not simple. Parenting deepens our powers to love and widens our commitment to justice; it also makes us fiercely protective of our own children, an instinct that all but obscures every other motive, value, and goal. Obviously, these two impulses do not always conflict. I can love my child deeply, want to do the best by her, and also fight for a world in which the social structures allow everyone to have the opportunities I forge for her.

But we cannot avoid real tensions. For many parents, the conflict arises over issues of time, energy, and focus. Do we spend Saturday taking our children to the zoo or working in a soup kitchen? On the one hand, I recall the apocryphal story of the son of a social worker who said, "I wish I were a poor kid so my mom would spend a full hour with me." On the other hand, when I asked Daphne, a ten-year-old, if her father really believed in his religion, she answered proudly, without missing a beat, "He sure does! Every other Sunday he goes with our church to build houses for homeless people." That is when religion gets real, and kids know it. And they are watching us.

The most difficult version of that conflict is the question of risk. You may know people who have been arrested and spent time in jail for civil disobedience, people who have lost their job for speaking out against an immoral policy, people who have chosen to enter dangerous situations in order to lend their support. But you probably know fewer parents of young children—especially mothers—who have done those things.

Noah, who had been a great risk taker as a young man and was again quite daring when his children were grown, said, "I devoted a certain number of years to raising my children. During that time I did less than I might have on social issues, but I believed in the Hindu conception that life is to be led in stages and that different activities are appropriate to different stages." For some parents, the idea of "living in chapters" (as Elton Trueblood calls it) helps them through.

In the end, we can hope that our kids will grow up to be the kind of people who will have the motivation, talents, and opportunities to address some of the injustice we leave uncorrected. And here is one more paradox. In our work in the world to make it a better, fairer place, the demands of our children hold us back. But the children we influence and leave behind—also fallible, also mortal—can continue some of that work for just a little while longer.

Chapter 11

BATH TIME

Forgiveness

"What if children were not washable?"

Most adults don't think much about baths. We usually take showers to get clean, and that is the end of the matter. Children challenge that utilitarian perspective. For the parents of small children, baths have only a little bit to do with getting children clean and a lot to do with the actual process of giving a bath. It is an integral part of the cycle of the day. Parents speak not about a "bath" but about "bath time." It is a time for soaking away the stains of the day (or sometimes the week), watching our children becoming clean, fresh, and pure once again. As we wash away our children's grime, we can let ourselves believe that our hearts, too, may become clean again.

We begin our lives floating in the waters of the womb. According to the biblical creation story, the primeval waters are gathered together into what Genesis 1:10 calls a *mikvah*. Since we originate in water in two different ways, it is no wonder that from ancient times a convert to Judaism had to be immersed in a pool of water—called a *mikvah*—in order to be reborn as a Jew. Later, Christians transformed this rite into baptism. So for a very long time, water has been the medium for birth and rebirth, beginning and beginning again.

Take a filthy child and put her in the tub, and eventually you will remove a clean one. "Did you ever consider how difficult life would be," asks S. Adams Sullivan, the author of *The Quality Time Almanac*, "if children's skin were no more washable . . . than . . . a pair of sneakers?" Then consider: we could have been so constituted that we never changed. If we felt angry, we would always feel angry; if we hurt, we'd always hurt; if we had a falling out with someone, we could never be friends again. But happily, that isn't the way we are made. Souls are washable. Children, in particular, remind us of our capacity for change because they move so rapidly from one mood to the next, cleaning up their emotional messes as easily as they create them.

Children do this daily, but especially in baths. One thing is clear. Children often can forget their sins and ours as rapidly as hot water removes large quantities of peanut butter and jelly from their faces and hair. Seeing children's ability to change makes some parents realize that change is possible for them as well. Watching how quickly children can give up anger and moods helps us loosen our grip on our own hurts and worries.

The average child is probably "given" about 1,800 baths by the time he is six. If each time we gave a bath we thought about the wonder of washability, how strongly the reality of renewal would grow in us! Giving children baths has no sacramental status in any religion I know of, but it can be a powerful opportunity for awareness. We need to work each day on our sense that transformation is possible.

Children teach us about forgiveness, first by being forgiving themselves. Gail, like most parents, cannot believe how quickly her child can move from insults to hugs. One night when Gail served dinner later than usual, her six-year-old was out of sorts and whiny. He complained about everything and broke all the rules of proper table behavior. Finally, Gail sent him in tears to his room. He slammed the door yelling, "I hate you all." After dinner, she went up and found him sprawled across his bed, fast asleep. Gail tossed and turned all night, guiltily replaying the scene in her mind. But the next morning, there was her son at her bedside, smiling happily and wondering, "Do you want to hear a neat riddle?" It wasn't that he had forgotten the incident; it is just that for him, it was completed.

Children are also forgiving of others. Samantha told me about a conversation she had with her four-year-old, Amanda. Every day as they drove out of their neighborhood, they passed a grumpy-looking older man sitting on his stoop. Amanda would wave cheerily from the window; the man would not respond. Amanda kept asking her mother, "Why won't that man wave to me?" Samantha responded that she really did not know. But Amanda persisted. "Why?" Samantha expected Amanda to get angry with the man, but instead, Amanda came to her own resolution of the problem. "It isn't his fault," she decided. "He must be handicapped in his heart."

Children teach us a matter-of-fact acceptance of the world as it is. Reba's husband was dying of cancer and had moved from their home to a hospice. Several weeks later, Reba took their one-and-a-half-year-old son Sidney to visit his father. She was worried: Would her husband be able to respond the way Sidney hoped? Would Sidney be frightened by his father's appearance? Although there was hardly a question of "fault" here, Reba was afraid Sidney might be angry at his father, if he recognized him at all.

But her fears proved unfounded. The minute Sidney saw his dad in a wheelchair at the end of the hall, he shouted out joyously, "Daddy! Daddy!" Sidney's love for his father could see right past the physical changes. Sidney saw the essence, not the externals, and his love was unconditional.

We also learn about forgiveness when we find ourselves forgiving our children. Brenda recalls a particular incident of "murderous rage" toward her son, Dan. "We were hiking, and seven-year-old Dan ran out ahead of the group on the trail," recalls Brenda. "He came to a long, slippery log stretched across a creek three feet below, and as we came around the bend, there he was rather nonchalantly walking across this mossy log. I was just furious. How could he be so stupid? He could break his neck! I wanted to throttle him. Instead I began to scream.

"Of course, within seconds, I realized that was the worst thing I could possibly do. My screaming might frighten him and cause him to fall. I needed to call upon every ounce of strength and patience within me to handle this in a way that would keep Dan safe. Suddenly it hit me. I was so angry only because I loved him so much. I wanted to kill the kid because I was afraid he might die. The whole incident turned around. I looked at Dan again. This time, instead of seeing a cocky, impudent brat, I saw this terrific kid full of his power, taking on the world with joy. The son who swaggered fearlessly onto that log making me so furious also made me so proud.

"Once Dan was safe again, I held him tight and cried. I told him how much I loved him. He was growing into a courageous young man. It was my job to teach him to combine his courage with caution. I told him I had been extremely angry but that I was not angry anymore. I had found the recipe to heal future blowups: if in the heat of anger I could call up my love for this child, the love that fueled my caring enough to be this angry, then I could respond appropriately and, more important, move on."

Some parents also experience forgiveness flowing in the other direction— toward their own parents. Parenthood gives them new humility, new compassion, a new ability to understand and forgive other parents in general and their own parents in particular. Marvin observed, "I was pretty judgmental before I had kids. It was easy then to see what parents were doing wrong. But now that I know how hard it is to make the right decisions, how tired you are, I am much more generous in my evaluations of others."

Vicki told me how her mother never had time for her when she was growing up. "When I left home, I was still very angry at my mother. There was just so much that I felt I never got from her. Even later, when I understood all the valid reasons why my mother had so little to give at that point in her life, I could not let go of my hurt." Vicki's heart finally softened toward her mother when Vicki had a child. "At that point my mother was in a position to give energy and caring to my baby." The first time Vicki returned from leaving her baby with her mom, she saw them playing together through the window. She began to cry. When she stopped crying, she realized that something dramatic had shifted within her.

Joanie forgave her mother when she found herself in the identical situation her mother was in—and acted differently. "My grandmother was an Orthodox Jew, an immigrant to this country. When my mother menstruated for the first time, she ran to her mother to tell her the news. My grandmother said not a word but simply slapped my mother across the face. Apparently, this is an old Jewish custom. My mother was hurt, not physically but emotionally. So when I came to her with the news of my first period, although she was tempted to slap me, she did not lift a hand. Instead, she told me the story of how her mother had hit her. Unfortunately, the story had almost as much effect as being hit. I still spent my adolescence wondering about the slap I did *not* get. I resented my mother for telling me the story at all.

"The moment of truth came when my daughter got her period for the first time. I felt not the slightest urge to hit her, but I did feel the words of the story rising in my mouth. I came within an inch of telling her the story my mother told me. I swallowed hard. I realized that not only would I not slap my daughter but through an act of will—much like my mother's in not slapping me—I would not even tell her the story. Now that I knew how easy it would have been for me to do what my mother did, I was impressed with my mother's courage in breaking free from *her* past. She had made it possible for me to take the next step. Further, now that I knew that I did not have to do what my mother did, I was suddenly full of love and gratitude to her for beginning a process which I continued."

Sometimes we can forgive our parents and our children simultaneously. Stella remembered the moment her heart softened twice: a double forgiveness. She was in her parents' house with her brother. Although Stella and her brother were both parents themselves, they still could go at it on occasion. At this particular moment, she was furious with him. She was just about to unleash a torrent of sarcasm when she noticed her mother watching from the kitchen table. The look of sheer pain in her mother's face was strikingly familiar. It was Stella's pain, the pain she felt every day as she watched and listened to her own son and daughter fight. It was so awful to see two people she loved so much hurt each other. At that moment it hit her: that was exactly how her mother must be feeling!

She clammed up, stopping the fight before it got under way. She wanted to put her arm around her mother and say, "Don't take it so hard. We really love each other. It's just that siblings are safe targets. They are so ready at hand, so available, it is easy to try out different emotions, to let go of some of the constraints we have with people who are more distant."

At that moment, she felt warm and loving toward her long-suffering mother whose pain she now knew. She could even forgive the intolerant way her mother had handled those fights when she and her brother were small. She understood her mother's rage.

She also felt a flood of love and forgiveness toward her children. Everything she had wanted to say in her own defense was true, and she could see that her children were, indeed, doing the best they could. Having forgiven both her mother and her children, Stella felt great. She realized that forgiveness is not something you do for the people you are mad at; it is a gift to yourself. It frees you from carrying around the hurt any longer, from being the victim. A person who can forgive easily finds life less painful. Parents try to teach their children how to be forgiving people not only because it is a "virtue" but because parents want their children to enjoy their lives.

I find it possible to forgive my children (once the angry moment has passed) and have been able to forgive my own parents. But what I find most difficult as a parent is forgiving *myself*. While I have made many mistakes in my life—at work, in relationships, in taking care of myself—the mistakes that hurt the most are those I have made with my children. I feel that I have betrayed a trust. Parenthood has evoked for me, more than anything else in my life, a sense of needing forgiveness.

In fact, guilt was my problem in the only interview I could not complete. Rhonda was married for twenty years before she had her child. She was a teacher, and a good one. For the first decade of her marriage, she did not want children. Then she had trouble conceiving. Finally, at the age of forty she gave birth to her one and only child, a healthy girl named Claire. Rhonda had done a huge amount of reading during her pregnancy and had made certain basic decisions about how she wanted to raise Claire. First, Claire would nurse as long as she wanted, when she wanted, till whatever age she wanted. Second, at night, Claire would sleep with her mother and nurse at will. Third, Rhonda would leave Claire as infrequently as possible until she was four. When Claire was old enough to understand separation without anxiety, Rhonda would consider possible group activities for her. Of course, Rhonda was investigating home schooling.

When I met Rhonda, Claire was two and a half. Mother and daughter had rarely been apart. The nursing was still going strong. As I sat and tried to conduct the interview professionally, I found it increasingly difficult to ask appropriate questions or to type the answers.

Instead, my mind filled with memories. There was the first time Seth and I left our child and went to the movies alone. I fled in the middle after a scene in which someone milked a cow. All through the scene I was sure I heard cries (fifteen city blocks away) and that they were for me. There were the nights I lay in bed listening to my daughter crying in the next room in her crib while I read and reread *Helping Your Child Sleep Through the Night*. The author, Dr. Farber, said the baby would only cry for a few nights, at the most two weeks. Mine cried for three. Every farewell, every tear came flooding back and literally overwhelmed me with guilt. An inner dialogue began.

MY RATIONAL SELF: *You could never have slept in a family bed or stayed home all day when your girls were small.*

MY EMOTIONAL SELF: *But maybe I should have.*

MY RATIONAL SELF: *Look. Parents have different styles. What this woman does is extreme. Why can't you just listen to this story without feeling personally threatened? She's not telling you her way is the only way. Every mother who makes choices about work and children is constantly looking over her shoulder at the road not taken. It's a sickness. In our culture right now, it's an epidemic!*

I realized that this internal dialogue was taking so much energy that I could not focus on the interview. Nor could I ring a buzzer to end the debate in my head. So I ended the interview.

I now know I am not alone in feeling guilt as a parent. When I was showing drafts of this chapter to some friends, I learned how prone to remorse parents—particularly mothers—can be. Although this chapter is about forgiveness, it seemed to have the paradoxical effect of inducing guilt. On reading it, several mothers reported the same reaction: they felt guilty that they did not give their children more baths! On a deeper level, some friends with grown children shared with me a sense of regret evoked by this book. Said one, "I felt sorry that I hadn't done more when my children were younger to encourage their spiritual lives." Guilt seems so pervasive a part of parenting, it is no wonder that this chapter is among the longest in the book.

What helps parents with guilt? Friends, especially older ones, can provide saving perspective. Isabel told me about a visit from an older friend that changed her life as a mother. One day, Isabel had just put her baby in his upstairs crib and had sat down in the kitchen for a much-needed cup of tea and a chat with her friend. At the first squeak from the Fisher-Price intercom, Isabel, as usual, leaped to her feet. Her friend leaned over and turned off the machine. "What are you doing?" Isabel cried. "I read a study that *proved* that children during the first nine months should be responded to promptly. They actually cry less that way."

"I read that study too," her friend said calmly. "But you need this cup of tea. You had better balance your needs with the studies, or you will be dead before this kid enters nursery school."

Sometimes, it is precisely in dealing with our children that we learn to forgive ourselves. Marianne told me this story about a giant meltdown of anger: "My seven-year-old was always losing things. One day we were on our way out the door to school, and I asked her where her mittens were. I had already bought her three pairs that winter. She wasn't sure, although she *thought* she might know where *one* was. I completely lost it! How could she have lost *another* pair of mittens? I started to make caustic jokes—I'll have to take out a second mortgage to keep you in mittens—but what I really was saying in a thinly veiled way was 'You are an incompetent, disorganized slob, and I can't stand you.'

"Of course, she heard my real message loud and clear—you are no good. She was crying and crying. And I had to stop myself and think, What is going on here? Do I really believe a seven-year-old is a bad person because she can't keep track of her mittens? Of course not. So why am I saying that? Because that's what my mother said to me. That's the tape that is playing in my brain. And I believed it. Even now when I lose my gloves (several times already this winter, come to think of it!), I really *do* think I am a bad person. But I'm not bad—no more than my daughter is. It is just a bad tape.

"I was so thrilled by the realization that I wasn't the awful person I had always thought I was that I began to smile happily," remembers Marianne. "My daughter, still crying and feeling horrible about herself, looked at me, glowing like a fool, and stopped crying to stare in amazement. Why did Mommy look so joyous if she had this horrible child? I explained to her that I had just realized that I was a much better person than I had thought all these years and that she was a pretty wonderful person for helping me to realize it. She seemed satisfied, and went happily off to school with two mismatched mittens."

I thought this story was powerful because it was about the kind of healing revelation that sometimes comes when we temporarily lose control. At moments like this (and children provoke so many), the insight seems to come from a source beyond our busy brains. At the risk of gilding the lily, I couldn't resist adding a bit of crafted insight to her gut experience. "There is a postscript to your story, don't you see?"

Marianne looked at me blankly. I asked her, "What do you think *your* mother was doing when she excoriated you in those damaging ways so many years ago?"

Marianne smiled. "I guess she was doing what her mother did to her. Just playing her mother's tape. Now that you mention it, when her mother was a little girl, losing her mittens probably *was* a catastrophe. I remember my grandmother telling me how she was so poor as a child that when the cat ate a dollar bill, the family went into serious mourning for a week.

"I guess," she concluded, "when my mother was a little girl they may not have had TV yet, but they sure had mental tape recorders." So the story turned out to be about forgiving her mother as well. Once you pull on one strand of the web of hurt, the whole thing begins to unravel.

Sometimes, however, parents feel deep and long-lasting remorse for real suffering they cause their children. Jed came to me seeking rabbinical counseling. He had recently been through a harsh and acrimonious divorce. "I really should have had more therapy *before* I had children," he confessed. "I definitely did not learn everything I needed to know in kindergarten! One of the most shameful memories of my life is the night I left my marriage for good. I was really out of control, screaming and yelling at my wife, saying things I wish now I had never said. Just as I was about to slam the front door, I looked back to see my twelve-year-old daughter standing at the top of the stairs. I didn't know how long she had been standing there, but the look on her face told me she had heard plenty.

"I have gotten my own life in order now, and my daughter is doing well too. But I cannot stop thinking about her face that night—the pain, the disappointment, the real sense of betrayal. I have not been able to forgive myself, and I am afraid I never will."

It was clear to me that Jed had done everything humanly possible to repent. He had spent many difficult hours repairing his relationship with his ex-wife and his daughter. If confronted with the same situation again, he would handle it better. He had asked for and received the forgiveness of the people involved. Now he needed to forgive himself. I believe that the moment of true remorse, of true desire to repent, is one of the deepest moments of our lives, one when we are most fully authentic. I told him he was touching the most fearless, the most genuine place in himself as he longed for forgiveness.

I also told him that I believe forgiveness, beyond all the interpersonal work we must accomplish, is ultimately a miracle, an act of grace for which we can only pray. When parents need forgiveness, they often turn to resources outside themselves. Catholicism has an ongoing discipline of confession. I encouraged Jed to use the upcoming days of repentance, culminating in Yom Kippur, as a time to seek "atonement."

Each year, as summer turns to fall, we rabbis tell our congregations that they too can turn a corner in their lives and let the past go. When I first began rabbinical work, this seemed to me to be asking a lot of people. I knew I was asking a lot of myself. It is tough facing what is deepest and truest inside ourselves and admitting we haven't always or even usually acted from that place, admitting our reckless treachery to our best selves, our fierce loyalty to our worst impulses. Every year as I reviewed my own misdeeds, I wished not only that I hadn't done them but that I were, in essence, the sort of person to whom it would never *occur* to do them. But I was not.

It was enough to make me suspect that the pagans were right, that life is all about endlessly recurring cycles and that Judaism merely taunts us when it teaches about a line that one can reverse and then follow through to a new and better self and world. To believe that it is really possible to change, to leave the old muck behind forever, was an enormous stretch for me.

Many people come to synagogue only on Yom Kippur. This seems to me like missing all of elementary school, then dropping in on a graduate seminar. Most of the year in synagogue we practice the ABCs: thankfulness, hope, moral duty. But this is the hard stuff: turning around, letting go of hurt inflicted and hurt sustained; having the courage to face once again the same list of sins in the prayer book, knowing that we did it last year—worse still, knowing we'll have to repeat the process next year—and still be able to pray, to try to turn. Yet this is the day that synagogues have standing room only.

Parenting may make it easier for us to understand this process.

Several years ago, just before the Day of Atonement arrived, I read in the newspaper about a sixties radical activist who had just surrendered to the police. She was wanted by the FBI for her part in the murder of a policeman, and she had lived underground for twenty-three years. Her parents—who hadn't seen or heard from her since the day they watched her on the evening news escaping from the shooting—were asked by reporters how they felt about their reunion with their child. They said simply, "We're her parents." What more was there to say?

The issue was not blame or forgiveness. What mattered most was the reunion itself, the connection, the homecoming. That's what would matter to me if my child were far away and in trouble. And that, I believe, is what matters to God.

When I saw that article, I knew why we chant a hymn entitled "Our Father, Our King" in preparation for the Day of Atonement. It is a prayer in which we call on God as our parent (in our synagogue we sing "Our Mother, Our Queen" as well). The ritual of confessing our sins presumes the unconditional, unqualified, nonnegotiable love of a mother or father for a child. And I also knew why, since becoming a parent, Yom Kippur had made more and more sense to me. Because of my children, I knew what it meant to love unconditionally, and I could finally experience that love for myself as well. Ultimately, I agree with my friends who say that

God is the love with which we forgive. We know this love to be real through our love for our children and their love for us. Although I have not experienced it, I expect that a similar process goes on for Catholics in the confession of sins. Perhaps this is part of the reason priests are called "Father."

The psalmists surely believed we could be forgiven. One spoke about it in the language of the bath:

> *Wash me thoroughly from my iniquity*
> *And cleanse me from my sin. . . .*
> *Create me a clean heart, O God,*
> *And renew a steadfast spirit within me. (Ps. 51)*

Experiencing the washability of skin and of spirit is perhaps one of the aspects of life that most affirms our sense that our time here has meaning. In the difficult dynamics of family life, we learn that we can "become new." When we know forgiveness in a family, we know that the universe is at least hospitable to our search for healing.

In the Christian tradition, forgiveness is central. "How many times should you forgive?" the disciples asked Jesus. And he responded, "Seventy times seven." Parents might want to double that number, for there is so much forgiveness waiting to happen. Our children may need to forgive us; we may need to forgive them, forgive our parents, forgive ourselves. And yet it is the ongoing grace of family life that it can happen.

At this point, you might assume that my children love to take baths. After all, baths are such a rich spiritual metaphor. But that's the tricky part about kids. The metaphor may be great, your ideas may inspire others, but do your kids care? Just as I was completing this chapter, my seven-year-old decided that she *hated* taking baths. And so the bath became a nightly (OK, a weekly) struggle. That is one of the great challenges and strengths of writing theology based on parenting. It keeps me humble. I can't take any of my ideas too seriously. My children won't let me.

Chapter 12

STORY TIME

Meaning

"God created human beings because God loves stories."

When Gina was growing up, she and her brothers trooped over to Grandma's house every night after dinner. There among their cousins, all clad in pajamas, they sat around the fire as Grandma read to them from the Bible, from Charles Dickens, from the great poetry of the world. It was the spiritual center of their day. Today, most families are too busy to build fires and read long books on a daily basis. Still, the old custom persists in new ways. Some families read aloud on long car trips when everyone is a captive audience. Other families share stories through watching videos together. Still others make space for reading poetry or special texts on holidays. And many, many families, especially those with young children, still practice the time-honored rite of the bedtime story.

Even in families that observe no other rituals, one often emerges: each night at more or less the same time and place, parent and child read a story. Bonnie has read to her son every night for ten years, since he was one. "I work long hours and my son is in school and then after-school care. In the evening, there is dinner, then homework, then violin practice. The highlight of the day is story time. I come to my son's bed in the last minutes before he goes to sleep, and I read him a chapter from a book. Even though I am sometimes so tired that I fall asleep midparagraph, we still cherish the time together."

Whether the stories begin in books, comics, videos, or parents' heads, whether they are told in bed, in the living room, or in a car, they are more than just a way to pass the time. Story is one of what Joseph Campbell calls the "masks of God." Narrative theologians explain in fancy language what primitive people, children, and parents already know. Before there were dogmas and rules, there were stories. Fundamental to any religion, any life, is the shaping of raw experience through story, giving narrative form and meaning to events. Stories provide a structure for understanding the world.

My mother and father are sometimes asked what their four grown children do for a living. They reply with pride that they have one rabbi, one clinical psychologist, one movie producer, and one TV director. On the surface, these careers may seem quite different from each other, but to me it seems clear that all four of us are basically in the same business. Just as our grandfathers on the Lower East Side started out peddling their products (one was in floor covering, one in furs), we are all in the story business. I preach and teach ancient Jewish stories, my sister listens as people tell her their stories, and my brothers make stories come alive for their audiences. We all believe that our lives are stories, that living a good life means telling a good story with it, and that stories heal.

How do stories heal? First, they show us we are not alone. I love to retell a famous story from the most ancient Buddhist tradition. The way I tell it, it is a story about the healing power of stories. A woman came to the Buddha with her dead child on her hip. "Give me medicine!" she cried. "I have been all around the town, and my burden is growing heavy. I have been told that only the Buddha can provide the medicine I need."

The Buddha gave her the following instructions: "Go from house to house, and in each home where no one has died, obtain a few small bits of mustard seed. Then bring them back to me."

The woman knocked on the first door and explained her mission. The man inside was happy to provide some mustard seed, but alas, his wife had just died. He told her all about what had happened. And so it went in one house after another. Each family had a story of some sorrow, some loss. Finally, the woman buried her son at the outskirts of the town and returned to the Buddha empty-handed, ready to move on. Indeed, the healing that comes from feeling part of a great kaleidoscope of stories is an important part of what this book is all about.

Stories can help parents and children see their lives in perspective, sometimes through humor. One mother told me about Judith Viorst's classic picture book, *Alexander and the Terrible, Horrible, No Good, Very Bad*

Day. Her children had heard the book often, and it gave them a resource for dealing with their own troubles. When one of them came home discouraged over things that had gone wrong at school, the parents would joke, "I bet you had a Terrible, Horrible, No Good, Very Bad Day." The literary allusion shifted the focus. The child's woes were no longer unique affronts to his spirit but part of the buffeting of the human condition that he, like Alexander, would have to learn to endure with relatively good cheer. (Parents also have days like Alexander's and find he helps give them perspective too.)

The humorous Mrs. Piggle-Wiggle volumes also helped several families I met. Mrs. Piggle-Wiggle is a freelance wisewoman who solves intractable child-rearing problems for the neighborhood. If a child refuses to take a bath, her prescription is to *forbid* the child to bathe and then plant radish seeds on his dirty skin. (I believe psychologists now call this paradoxical intervention.) One older parent recalled, "Some of our happiest family memories revolve around reading that book aloud. We all laughed and laughed. More important, when one of the kids was misbehaving—refusing to go to sleep, for example—the rest of us would remind him of Mrs. Piggle-Wiggle's solution, *forcing* him to stay awake until he dropped. The silliness would deflect the power struggle long enough for the kid to do the right thing."

Stories also provide emotional catharsis. One mother told me a story about her family viewing a video together. "My husband and I and my two daughters climbed into our big double bed one Friday night to watch *A League of Their Own*," she recalled. "It is a movie about a women's professional baseball league during World War II. Watching let all of us be physically close and do something together at the end of a long, busy week—without a great deal of effort.

"We all enjoyed the movie. In the last scene, the two sisters find themselves playing on opposing teams in a big, important game. The younger sister, who has always been jealous of the older one, hits what could be a home run. As she runs toward home plate, the ball is thrown to the catcher—her sister. She slides into home at the very moment her sister catches the ball. She knocks her sister over and the sister drops the ball.

"At the moment when the big sister fell to the ground and the little sister had her triumph, my younger daughter began to cry hard. She wept and wept. It lasted about twenty minutes. We all took turns holding her as she sobbed. For her, this was not just a story. It allowed her to play out an emotional drama—wanting to beat her older sister, terrified at seeing it happen—in a safe way. It was a very precious, sacred kind of time."

Stories also allow children to face down their fears—at their own pace. One mother told me about her daughter watching *Dumbo* at the age of two and a half. "She would call me into the room when it was time for the scene where Dumbo is separated from his mother. She would make me skip over the scene with the VCR fast-forward button. Each time she watched it, she would let me skip less and less, as she could tolerate more and more. Soon, she was able to watch the whole scene, with me sitting there. What was so great was that she was able to experience exactly as much or as little as she was able to handle."

Vera, whose childhood had been disorganized to the point of chaos, said, "It was really important to me to read my daughter stories about little girls who live in an environment of great peace and order. That is what I find so appealing about the Madeleine books. The little girls may be orphans, but they know exactly where they fit in the two straight lines as they have their meals, go on their walks. I find it very comforting.

"Unfortunately," Vera continued (and here I knew what was coming), "unfortunately, my daughter does not *like* the Madeleine books, at least not that much. What she really loves are Maurice Sendak's *In the Night Kitchen* and *Where the Wild Things Are*. I find those books a bit bizarre, scary, and unsettling. But I read them to her anyway—over and over again. I figure she knows what she wants. I just go on automatic pilot and read, wishing I were reading *Madeleine*."

Several parents I interviewed talked about the extraordinary pull of the movie *Mary Poppins*. "Our daughter must have watched that movie thirty times during her first three years." Aside from finally answering a child's inevitable question—Where do those baby-sitters *come* from? (quite obviously, the sky!)—it fulfills the child's greatest fantasy: that someday, someone will magically appear who will make their family better.

Heddy's first daughter was six when her safe and secure world crumbled around her: her new baby sister was born with major health problems. Heddy knew her older daughter needed some safety zone where she could address her intense feelings about this earthquake in her family's life. So Heddy created the "Samantha stories." Samantha was a little girl whose family had the most extraordinarily bad luck. In one story, a tornado hit Samantha's house. In another, the family went boating and a thunderstorm swept the boat away. Each time, the family survived, stronger for the experience.

Heddy explained, "We all colluded in the fiction that this family had nothing to do with us, even though my daughter knew that she was the brave Samantha." The stories had certain elements that always repeated. At their core was a terrifying, unmanageable event that the family ultimately managed. Later, as a teenager having a difficult time, Heddy's daughter sometimes would ask wistfully, "Mom, do you think a Samantha story would work now?"

Stories help both children and adults deal with evil. Parents often try to pretty up stories for their children. Many described their initial shock when they realized that the classic fairy tales were actually quite violent stuff. I remember reading the original Grimm Brothers version of "Cinderella" aloud to my daughter and discovering in horror that the stepsisters cut off their toes to try to fit into the glass slipper. I quickly edited that part out as I read. In fact, when I told the story of the exodus from Egypt to my first child, I excised the ten plagues.

At some point, however, I finally realized there was a reason these dark-edged stories (including the Bible) had never gone out of print. Children crave scary stories. Children do not want stories that claim that evil does not exist. They know it does. They want stories that tell them that evil is ultimately weaker than good. In order to get that message across, the evil must be acknowledged. As one mother said, "Easter does not make any sense without Good Friday."

Sometimes parents need to help a child wrest order out of chaos. When Matthew's son was dying, Matthew felt helpless. One day, in a bookstore, he came across a book that recounted the stories of people who had had a near-death experience. Trembling, Matthew opened the book. To his relief, he discovered that the reports were comforting, inspiring, full of visions of light. Matthew bought the book and began reading the accounts to his son as he was falling asleep. Matthew had no illusions that his son would miraculously get better like the informants in this book. Nor was he entirely sure if actually dying would be the same as nearly dying. But he believed that these stories would help his son filter his own experience, impose a shape and structure on raw events.

My friend Tina Davidson, a well-known composer, learned that she required open-heart surgery to heal a nine-year illness. If the surgery were successful, Tina would be fine, but she might not survive the operation. There was so much Tina wanted to communicate to her only child, but her daughter was only six years old. So before she left for Cleveland, where the surgery would take place, Tina wrote and illustrated a book. It was about a little girl whose mother dies. An owl leads the girl to a large pearl that represents her mother's love. Even if the girl drops the pearl, it never breaks. The pearl is always available to her. Tina left the book in a place where she know her daughter would eventually find it. In fact, the surgery was a success, and the book remains unopened in a dresser drawer, a testament to Tina's belief in the power of imagery to communicate important truths.

While death cannot be vanquished by stories, telling stories can, in the words of a Jewish prayer, "avert the severity of the decree." One morning, as we sat at the breakfast table, I read in the newspaper that Dr. Seuss had died. I shared this information with the family. My three-year-old looked stricken and ran from the dining room. She returned a minute later smiling with relief. "They are still there!" she exclaimed. It took us a while to figure out that in her still magical mind, she had assumed that a person's death would automatically result in the disappearance of all his books from her bookshelf. She had found instead that although Dr. Seuss may have died, his stories would remain as long as she wanted to read them. What if a person's words just vanished from the earth the moment he died? How awful! Every day we laugh and cry over the words of people long dead. How amazing!

Stories can help heal the wounds of personal suffering. As a child, I learned this story: one Sabbath afternoon, Rabbi Meir came home from the house of study. His wife Beruriah greeted him, served him dinner, and watched him perform the ritual to conclude the Sabbath. Then she asked him, "A while ago, a man came to the house and left two jewels. Now he has returned and asked for his jewels back. Should I give them to him?"

"Of course," said the rabbi. "Anyone who keeps a pledge must return it to its rightful owner when he calls for it." Then Beruriah took her husband by the hand to their sons' bedroom where the boys lay still, having just died of a plague. Meir wept inconsolably, but his wife was calm. "Did you not tell me that we must return the jewels when their owner asks for them?"

As a rabbi, I would not think of telling that story at the funeral of a child, nor would I repeat it to someone who was mourning a death. It seems to me too facile, too serene to be helpful to a person at a time of great pain. But I have told that story to my children as a bedtime tale, an example of a wisewoman from long ago. That story now forms one small element of their worldview that may later come into play as they make meaning of their own struggles. To my mind, that story is an inadequate answer to the question of suffering. It is, however, a piece of a much larger imaginative picture of the world.

The story of Beruriah shows us both her ability to let go and her husband's ongoing pain. Parents find that their children's feelings are intense and that some are more acceptable than others. The stories told by religious traditions can remind parents how varied the emotional reactions to suffering can be. Stories are never perfect answers, but they allow us to ask the questions in different ways and to try on different responses.

Stories can sometimes help a child do what he needs to do. While one observer might call the following story a case of deception, another might call it entering the child's world of fantasy and story. Sylvia's son George was a boy who knew what he liked and did not like, and peeing in the toilet was not something he liked, at least not by the age of three. Rather than despairing, his mother tried to find out *why* he was so averse to using the toilet. Finally, she guessed. "Is it because you really wish you could save your pee?"

Sylvia had guessed right, but now what? On Saturday, she let him pee in bottles that they saved on the bathroom counter. But by Sunday, she knew she needed a different solution. She told George she would call the "toilet company" and arrange to have all his pee saved. She placed the "call" right in front of him. She explained to the toilet company that from now on, they needed to save all of George's pee. Then she put a sign on each toilet in their house, "Dear toilet company, Don't forget to save George's pee!"

The plan worked beautifully, with one hitch. George peed happily in all of the toilets in his home, but he still needed to wear a diaper to nursery school. So Sylvia went to the school and hung up a similar note on the school's toilet.

When George was eight, Sylvia reminisced with her son about the signs. George had come to suspect the whole thing had been a ruse, and he told her gently that he had figured it out. After she confessed, she asked, "Are you angry with me?" He was not in the least. It seemed he was touched that she had taken the trouble to enter his head, to see the world from his perspective, and create a fantasy that allowed him to join the grown-up world gracefully. Or as George put it: "It was fun."

Stories are also magic. One divorced mother told me about her experience taking her eight-year-old son to visit his father in California while she visited friends nearby. "It was a wonderful week for him," she told me, "and he was devastated about having to leave. Before the trip, he had gotten used to not having his dad, and now he had to get used to it all over again.

"On the way home in the airplane, he was whining and unpleasant. Since he always loved stories, I pulled out a book to read aloud. It was a library book that I had grabbed off the table on the way out the door to the airport, not focusing much on what I had brought. As I read aloud, I realized that *A Day of Pleasure* by Isaac Bashevis Singer was the autobiographical account of a very poor Jewish boy in Eastern Europe. Singer tells vignettes about his life filled with the sights, sounds, smells, and tastes of a pre–World War I Polish tenement.

"Together, my son and I plunged into a world of narrow, muddy roads and crowded courtyards filled with noise, a world of bearded rabbis and smoky locomotives and live geese and chicken squawking in the marketplace and street urchins and washerwomen with huge loads on their heads. Two hours later we were still there, in Warsaw, feeling the hunger imposed by wartime shortages, wishing for another kopeck so that Mother could buy the potatoes and onions and flour she needed for the daily soup.

"When the plane landed, it jolted us back to our reality. I realized, with not a little satisfaction, that we had just been on a ride more magical than any he had waited on line for at Disneyland. We had dwelt in another world with the help of nothing more expensive than a library card and our imaginations." When we are stuck in a not-very-satisfactory real world, stories can heal by creating an alternative world. That is indeed a kind of transcendence, a kind of miracle.

In a memoir, the author Salman Rushdie tells how he knew as a small boy what was worthy of respect, even of love—what was holy. "I grew up kissing books and bread. In our house, whenever anyone dropped a book or . . . a chapati . . . the fallen object was . . . kissed." Since Salman was clumsy as a child, he managed to kiss a fair number of books and quite a bit of chapati. As he put it, "One never forgets one's first loves."

In our house, books are not ritually kissed, but they are revered. We resort to books, as the marriage vows say, in sickness and in health, when we are happy or when we are sad. We believe books are "good for what ails you." One cold winter my daughter spent "a two-week vacation in Hawaii" by reading James Michener's long novel every day for two weeks. We kept urging her to come back to Philadelphia, but we had to admit the weather was better where she was. The daughter of a friend of ours has a surefire method for dealing with the blues. She climbs into bed with one of the novels in a four-part fantasy adventure series featuring a brave warrior woman. The family calls it "taking the Alana cure."

Families also tell their own stories, to give children a sense of their origins. Many tell stories in commemoration of an ancestor's birthday or death day, on special occasions like birth ceremonies, graduations, or weddings. Funerals, always a time to hear stories about the person who died, can become occasions to tell stories about the others whose graves are nearby or whose lives touched the newly deceased. In my work as a rabbi, nothing gives me more satisfaction than collecting material from a family for a eulogy. In this process, families share the stories of their relative's life and build a memorial out of words that allows their loved one to live on and helps them to move on.

Sometimes it is a challenge to create a rich legacy of family lore. From the outside, James had a typical middle-class suburban childhood. But inside, his home held dark secrets of mental illness and physical abuse. James left when he was fifteen to live on his own. He had broken the cycle of pain in his family, and he made a vow before he became a father that the hurting would stop with him. With his wife he has created a beautiful, loving home for himself and their daughter, who is now five.

Strangely, his daughter seemed drawn from the beginning to hearing stories about "the olden days." By this, she meant when her dad was a little boy. James had to search his childhood to find episodes that were, as he put it, "suitable for her consumption."

He went on to explain, "I basically had to edit my childhood. It was a good process. It forced me to focus on events that were less painful than the ones I had spent so much time in therapy discussing. In doing so, I actually ended up remembering some good moments, like the time my mother made me a great Halloween costume. True, those moments were few and far between, but they became more powerful in the retelling. The process gave me back my childhood in a better form." And doesn't that matter too? Not only the childhood we have had, but the story we choose to tell about it. That is our power as humans, to tell the story.

Finally, our children tell *us* stories. I grew up hearing about my great-grandmother Pearl, a woman of legendary status who came to America by herself at the age of eighteen and raised eight children. Though she never learned to read or write, she was wise and beloved, the ultimate mother. I never met Pearl, but I have frequently thought about her over the years, particularly while I was writing this book. I wished I had known Pearl and Pearl's stories. I wanted to hear the accounts of her younger days in Europe, the legends she had learned as a child, the fairy tales that she passed on to her children. I wanted to pass them on to mine.

So one day I set out for the Bronx to a nursing home to visit Pearl's only surviving child, my great-aunt Bertha. Fortunately, Bertha, at eighty-six, is still fully in control of her considerable mental faculties, still the intelligent, well-read, articulate person she always was. So, tape recorder in hand (I didn't want to trust my word processor on this one), I went to gather Pearl's stories.

Bertha remembered that just before all the children went to sleep, there was "story time." "My mother would come into our room and sit with us in the dark. We would talk a lot," she said.

"Great!" I exclaimed. "What were the stories she told you?"

"I can't remember any."

I was deflated.

But Bertha continued. "Now that I think about it, what happened during those evenings was that Mom listened and *we* talked. She wanted to hear *our* stories. She wanted to hear all about what happened to us every day, about what we were learning in school. Sometimes she was so tired that she would lie down in bed next to one of us and just listen. We taught her everything. She was eager to educate herself, and we were her vehicle for doing that. We went out into the world and brought back stories to her."

So I needn't have worried if Great-great-grandma Pearl's stories would prove of interest to my children. In order to pass down the tradition of Pearl, all I had to do was listen to my children's stories. And that could not fail to interest them.

As the novelist Elie Wiesel likes to say, "God created human beings because God loves stories."

PART 4

Night

Chapter 13

BEDTIME

Trust

"God is the open hand in which we rest as we go to sleep."

In all my years of studying religion in rabbinical school and graduate school, I never took a course in bedtimes. I never studied prayers said on the bed, deconstructed bedtime rituals, or discussed going to sleep as a serious religious event. I did learn that traditional Jews are supposed to say the *Shma* ("Listen, Jews, the Lord is God, the Lord is One") in bed at night because of the line in the Bible that reads, "You shall speak these words when . . . you lie down and when you rise up." Once, when perusing a traditional Jewish prayer book on my own, I came across a long night prayer that included this verse:

> *May the angel Michael be at my right hand,*
> *and Gabriel at my left,*
> *before me Uriel,*
> *behind me Raphael,*
> *and above my head the Divine Presence.*

I filed it away in the back of my brain and went on to study more lofty theological and metaphysical issues. I did not think about bedtime again. Until I had a child. At play group, I heard mothers comparing notes. "We have to read *Good Night, Moon*," said one. "Then we pull the covers up just so. Then there's the litany: 'Mommy loves you, Daddy loves you, Grandma loves you'. . . . When it's over we close the door, leaving just the right-size crack of light. Then, if we're lucky, he goes to sleep." I began to wonder, Do these kids take anthropology courses in ritual while in utero?

Kids just seem to *know*. Sleep is a realm where forces poorly understood, even by Freud, overwhelm us. Before we surrender to those dark recesses of our minds, slip into that other dimension in which we lack all control, we need to touch down first on the solid verities—or at least have an angel on each side of us. George Santayana spoke of religion's power to open the vistas for us to "another world in which to live." At bedtime, we want to gaze into that world before we lose our grip on this one.

When I began to talk to parents about bedtime, I discovered that I had chanced on the last frontier in secularism's conquest of modern life. Even people who never pray at any other time of the day or year offered stories of prayers with children at bedtime. Parents with no religious practices told me about ritualized back rubs, kisses, storytelling routines, and other stylized good nights that had the quality of holy time. More than one parent told me of fighting off sleep as she tried to induce it in her child through songs, stroking, and listening. Parents of older children reported that even when their kids got tough and unreachable, bedtime was still the vulnerable time—the time to get close, to share intimacy. While writing this book, I asked many children, What advice would you give parents who want to talk to their kids about religion? One twelve-year-old girl said, "Tell them to do it at bedtime. Kids will talk about *anything* rather than go to sleep."

But kids are not the only ones who need help with this nightly passage. I asked a child therapist about bedtimes. Whenever she works with a "troubled child," early in the treatment she discusses with the parents the question of when the child is put to sleep. Inevitably she discovers that the child goes to bed very late, much later than he ought to, much later than he, it turns out, even wants to. Why don't the parents make him go to sleep sooner? "I think they are so eager to be rid of him and so guilty about that feeling that they end up incapable of setting a limit on their time together. Especially when the day has not been a success, parents simply are not ready to separate yet."

Beyond the separation of parent and child, the best-known children's bedtime prayers give us a clue as to what is at issue in going to sleep. Many people in my generation were raised with a famous Christian prayer:

Now I lay me down to sleep,
I pray the Lord my soul to keep;
If I should die before I wake,
I pray the Lord my soul to take.

And most have heard at least snippets of the renowned seventeenth-century Scottish prayer:

From ghoulies and ghosties
And long-leggedy beasties
And things that go bump in the night,
May the good Lord deliver us.

Those prayers get right to the point. Most bedtime prayers and rituals, while not directly addressing the fear of dying in one's sleep or of "things that go bump in the night," do so subtly. The famous closing hymn of the synagogue liturgy, Adon Olam, was originally written by a medieval Spanish rabbi, most likely as a bedtime prayer. Surely the last verse of Adon Olam is one of the most apt night prayers imaginable:

In God's open hand I rest my soul
When I go to sleep, and when I wake,
And with my soul, this body, here.
God is with me; I shall not fear.

What people seemed to value about their own memories of childhood rituals was dependability. All agreed that the words mattered less than the performance, and the routine mattered most of all. People recalled the simple reliability that gave them a sense of being connected to something stable outside themselves. They needed this reassurance as they were about to be left alone for the night. Those who had experienced bedtime prayers and rituals wanted to pass them on to their children, sometimes surprisingly intact.

Sandy chose not to raise her children in an institutional religious faith. "I can meditate, I can think, but I don't know what people are talking about when they say they are praying. I'm perplexed and, quite honestly, jealous. I feel sorry for myself." Nevertheless, Sandy taught both of her children the simple prayer her parents had made her memorize and recite throughout her childhood:

Heavenly Father, now that the day is over and the quiet night has come, I ask you once again to forgive me for anything I have done wrong and to help me to do better tomorrow. Watch over my parents and all those I love so we can wake again to the pleasant morning light.

There are parts of the prayer she would have written differently had she been its author, but she never considered editing even a word before passing it on to her children. "I loved that prayer. Saying it every night during my whole childhood was a happy memory. So I wanted my children to say it too. I especially enjoyed the 'pleasant morning light.' It shaped my attitude toward waking up." Perhaps this is what Santayana meant when he spoke of the "special bias" a religion gives to life.

Allison grew up in a wealthy, assimilated Jewish household in Manhattan. Although she went to an elegant temple where she sat in a pew with her family name engraved on it, the only bedtime prayer she experienced was taught to her by her Christian governess. Many years later, Allison found herself alone at night in a hospital bed, facing a life-threatening operation the next day. To her amazement, she found herself reciting, "Jesus loves me, this I know." She derived immense comfort not from an alien theology that she disbelieved but from the evocation of a time of safety and of love.

Even for parents without connection to a religious tradition, bedtime is still an opportunity to reach out to "another world in which to live." They wisely intuit a need to make a fuss about bedtime. For some, music is the other world in which they feel safe. John, for example, wanted to be a folksinger when he was young. Instead, he became a corporate lawyer. Bedtime was music time for his two boys, now grown. He would arrive at their bedsides, guitar in hand, and play and sing for them all his favorite songs until they were both safely and soundly asleep. (In contrast, I am a rabbi who is living proof of the need for cantors. When my kids will not sleep, as a last resort I offer to sing to them. They immediately nod off . . . or at least pretend to.)

Meg uses the minutes just before sleep to share "dark time" with her six-year-old daughter, Zoe. Meg turns off all the lights and sits quietly on the edge of her daughter's bed. Within minutes, Zoe is sharing stories of the day and, on occasion, her deepest thoughts and feelings. Sometimes during the day Meg will ask Zoe a question and Zoe will respond, "I can't tell you about that until dark time."

The most effective child rituals are tangible. Some parents and children create a simple ritual out of the act of switching on the night-light. Others elaborate on the stuffed toy with whom the child sleeps. One book I read spoke about reciting, "The Lord is my shepherd, I shall not want," and supplementing the prayer with a stuffed lamb. Marta, a first-generation Mexican-American whose parents were "deeply anticlerical," never set foot inside a church after the family moved to the United States. The one remnant of religion that survived had to do with bedtime. Marta and her sisters each owned a treasured wooden crucifix that they brought with them when they emigrated. Marta would not think of going to sleep without "Papa Jesus" safely ensconced underneath her pillow.

My own bedtime ritual is both visual and tactile. Many years ago, I taught religion to students at a public university. I never forgot one of the term papers I received. The author, a young man who was Roman Catholic, recalled how each night his mother used to lift up the sheets high above his head and then let them billow gently down upon him until he was fully covered. Then he would fall off to sleep. I began doing the same thing with my daughter and added to the action a Hebrew prayer that said, "Spread over us your sukkah (canopy) of peace." For years, I put her to sleep saying that prayer and covering her with the falling sheets.

Sometimes I wondered, Is this all a giant enactment of the "whistle a happy tune" phenomenon in which parents who do not have any trust in the universe fool their kids into an illusion of safety so that the kids will go to sleep and the parents can have some free time in the evenings? I think it is more than that. *The ritual actually works.* Erik Erikson identifies the conflict between basic trust and mistrust as the very first "task of the ego." As he describes it, the successful resolution of this conflict depends mainly—if not entirely—on the quality of the parental (he refers to it as maternal) care the child receives in the first year of life. Yet the conflict is really lifelong, and the teaching often leads in the opposite direction, from child to parent.

Eva did not have a safe childhood. She was born in 1940 in Russia during a time of great instability. Her father was in a labor camp, and her mother scavenged food and tried to keep her daughter safe. There was neither bedtime nor ritual, much less bedtime ritual. Years later, in France, Eva became a mother. "It took a long time for me to have my first child, and the joy was immense. I achieved a sense of purpose and profound well-being. I was recreating myself and giving this child what I had missed. It was the best time of my whole life. Something or someone allowed me to have the family I never had." Her children nurtured her in a way that eased the hurt from her own childhood. "Having children was magical for me."

When her daughter was young, Eva sat each night on her daughter's bed and talked to her about the day that had passed, the day that was coming. Then they recalled the names of all their relatives and friends. No explicitly religious words were uttered. The official purpose of the custom, according to Eva, was to "situate her in time and space and a network of love." Eva continued, "It had the same effect on me. After a while, I began to realize the truth: tucking her in made *me* feel taken care of."

When Carol first discovered she was pregnant, she was terrified. She had absolutely no sense that she would be a good mother. Like many women pregnant for the first time, she worried constantly about the well-being of this child she could not even see or touch. Her anxiety and foreboding were compounded by her father Albert's terminal illness. Late in Carol's pregnancy, Albert died and the family was in chaos for several weeks. In the midst of the confusion, she was rushed to the hospital for an early, emergency C-section.

When the moment finally came and the baby was placed in her arms, alive and well, she felt—to her amazement—an immediate sense of peace. She offered her breast and the baby took it. Her first success! Parenting, while challenging, wasn't nearly as difficult as worrying about parenting had been! As she haltingly took each new step as a mother, she was constantly given immediate confirmation from a visible, vocal human being. She grew in confidence and trust, in herself and in the universe, through the process of watching her child grow.

And there was one more piece. She named her daughter Alice in memory of her father. "Before Alice was born, I felt like a toppling row of books with only one bookend—and that one had just been removed. With Alice, the second bookend was moved into place. But it was more than that. Naming her for my dad made it feel like the first bookend was back again as well. Even as a baby, Alice's gestures would remind me of him. Now I felt like a solid row of books held snugly upright on both ends."

We try to evoke trustfulness in our children at bedtime, but often it is they who teach us trust.

At bedtime, the act of one generation connecting to the other affirms that linear bond—what one mother called "verticalness"—that sense of security in being a link in a chain. When the parent learned the words of the bedtime ritual from her own parent, as in Sandy's case, the connection is even deeper. When the words come from an ancient tradition, the chain grows longer and also sturdier. But even the most simple act of reaching out from parent to child transforms what could be a frightening moment of separation into the seed of a "happy memory."

In that moment of connection, both generations gain access to another world in which to live, one populated by angels, one in which protection is a sure thing. I have no clue concerning the topography of that other world, although I've studied religious texts that purport to provide that information. I think that the prayers and quasi-prayers and rituals of bedtime are a mostly opaque window into a realm beyond our own. We cannot describe it, but perched on our children's beds, we can glimpse its reality.

Remember the last verse of Adon Olam, which speaks of going to sleep in God's hand? God is not an old man with a beard, a heavenly version of father Abraham, but an enormous outstretched, cupped hand. Earlier, the same hymn says, "God is my rock, my banner, my hiding place, the portion in my cup." The message is plain and clear: God doesn't protect us. God *is* protection. When we are stumbling on a hike and find a rock to grip, that rock is God. When we dream of waving a banner as we charge into battle with the "ghoulies and ghosties" of the night, God is the flag. When, running away from big sister, we find a safe hiding place in the back left of the basement closet, that cozy corner that we love is God. When every morning our cup is full of milk, God is our portion. The experience of putting a child to sleep is like the experience of the well-placed ledge on the trail. It says to us, Yes, the world is hospitable to your need for safety.

Some parents find bedtime one of their favorite parts of parenting. My own mother used to play a game in which I was the letter, the blankets were the envelope, and kisses on the forehead were the stamps. When we see our children sealed into bed secure and sound, we are not lying to them by telling them that they are safe. In fact, we strengthen our own faith in the basic security of the world by creating that experience for our children. Bedtime often becomes an hour of grace for parents. We can stop our own rushing and reach out through words and actions to the past, through our children to the future—in sum, to an eternity in which we are learning to trust, even in the most difficult circumstances.

My sister-in-law, Sarah, moved to Israel as a young woman and married an Israeli. Last Passover, Sarah's husband Shuki died of cancer, leaving her with two sons, ages one and three. This Passover, Sarah brought her children to America to visit us. She had business to do and left the boys with us for a week. When she returned, she asked her four-year-old if he had trouble falling asleep without her there. "Yes," he answered, "but only for a little while. Then I felt you coming into my heart, and I felt God patting me on the head."

I thought that was a wonderful response, and I told Sarah so. But what I really wanted to know was Sarah's reaction. "How did you feel when he said that?"

Sarah smiled. "I felt like God was patting me on the head."

Chapter 14

SLEEP

Separation

"When I get big, you and Daddy will live in my house."

It was our first date since we'd become parents. On arriving at the movie theater, we missed our infant daughter so much we called home to make sure everything was OK. As I dialed our number, the baby-sitter had just lulled her to sleep. The ringing of the telephone promptly undid that accomplishment. Hearing cries in the background, I hung up and let the baby-sitter begin her work again. Twenty minutes later, anxious to know if she had succeeded, Seth called back, just in time to wake the newly sleeping baby for the second time.

Is it any wonder separation is so hard for parents and for children? We are programmed to want to stay together. During the first few years of a human life, if the parent doesn't remain close to the baby or find a reliable substitute, the child will die. In the beginning, fusing is adaptive, natural. For an adult, after a lifetime of separateness, that depth of connection can feel quite wonderful. Then we have to begin to let go.

I once heard an anthropologist describe a tribe where separation is handled with a tidy ritual. For the first five years, the child sleeps with his mother on her mat and spends all day with her gathering berries. They never part. On the child's fifth birthday, the mat is burned, and the child joins the adult world. Everything is clear-cut.

In our society, separation begins earlier, takes longer, and is full of ambiguity. From an evening with a baby-sitter to day care, to school, to camp, to leaving home and establishing an adult identity, the process continues, year by year, well into adulthood. Bruno Bettelheim tells of a group of children at a preschool who, witnessing one of their friends sobbing over his mother's departure, ceased playing happily and started to cry, "I want my mommy." One of the teachers, who was also the mother of one of the crying boys, admonished her son, "There's no need for *you* to be upset. I'm right here." At which point the little boy promptly began to cry, "I want my daddy!"

Separation grief is not so much about the loss of a particular individual at a particular moment. It is also about all the partings that have gone before and all that will be in the future. That was true for the little boy in Bettelheim's story just as it is for many parents.

For more and more of us, separation begins early, when the child is first left at day care. The professionals agree that the parent's own attitude of relaxation and confidence is crucial for a smooth separation at the day-care door. But as I read their pronouncements in child-care manuals, I often wondered if the experts know how it feels from the parent's point of view. I decided to interview a professor of child development who was also a mother.

Marsha Weinraub of Temple University had taught child psychology for over fifteen years; her field of specialization was separation. Then she had a son. When he was five months old, she took him to a day-care center for the first time. She had observed this scene hundreds of times through a one-way mirror at the laboratory at her university. She had written articles and given lectures and knew all the right things to say and do. She knew the difference between "departure protest" and "distress." She was, after all, a professional.

"My research for my dissertation shows that it is important for the parent not to hesitate," she began.

"What did you do?"

"I hesitated."

She went on. "My research also shows that when parents are leaving children in excellent care, it does the children no harm and may even be good for them."

"So you left the building all smiles?"

"I cried."

The separation scholar–turned–mother did have some advantages over the rest of us. Even in her suffering, she knew this experience would help her teach parents about this matter with more empathy and integrity.

Moreover, she knew how to take care of herself. After leaving her child's classroom, she stopped into the day-care center director's office for some tender loving care.

Some parents discover that ritual can help them through this transition. Elise would always kiss her child in the same place behind the ear and make an elaborate set of instructions: "If you miss me, if you need to feel me, just touch the kiss." Gladys would take one key off her key chain and tell her son, "You can put this in your pocket, and anytime you want you can put your hand in and know it is there. It is the key to my heart." These rituals, Gladys and Elise both agreed, comforted the moms at least as much as they helped the children.

In Latin American countries, Catholic parents will make the sign of the cross on a child's forehead as they leave their presence. Clara, a Mexican-American mother, always did that for her children. Once, distracted by conversation, Clara simply said, "God be with you, have a good day," and her three-year-old son tugged at her arms and would not relent until she had crossed him. Vanessa Ochs, the author of *Safe and Sound: Protecting Your Child in an Unpredictable World,* recalls how her grandfather would give his grandchildren money to be donated to a beggar when they set out on trips. The theory was that no harm would befall the person engaged in a journey that was now for the purpose of fulfilling a commandment. But even more important, explains Ochs, the custom distracted her grandfather long enough for him to allow his beloved grandchildren the space to leave.

What is so hard about leaving our children? First, it is about giving up control. Whenever I leave my children, I think of the way I used to bowl as a child. Even after the bowling ball had left my hands and was rolling down the lane, I could not relinquish the hope of controlling matters. I would shout to the ball, blow at it, and wave my hands wildly in hopes of influencing its course. The ball, however, was well on its way already (usually heading for the gutter), oblivious to my spells.

A story about my paternal grandmother may explain the lineage of my instincts, if not justify them. When my father and his brother were young boys, they set out one Sunday from their apartment in the Bronx for a day at Yankee Stadium. When they arrived at their seats in the bleachers, they realized that their bag lunches were sitting on the kitchen table back home. Or so they thought. As they resigned themselves to their growling stomachs and became engrossed in the game, their mother was walking row by row through the hundreds of bleachers, lunches in hand, calling their names.

Some parents today have the same difficulty my grandmother did with separation. Dana told me this story: "We had just left my oldest daughter, age ten, at overnight camp for the first time. We stopped at a lake near the camp to enjoy the scenery. I stood there, staring at the water, feeling like I was going to faint. We got back in the car and turned on the news. It was 102 degrees, and it was still ten o'clock in the morning.

"For the next two weeks (the entire length of the camp), the temperature never went below one hundred. As I sweated through the days, I thought of my precious, vulnerable child, only thirty miles away, equally hot, and with no air-conditioning! One day at the swimming pool I met a woman whose daughter was at the same camp. She told me she had sent her child to camp with a small, battery-operated fan.

"Abandoning my plans for a swim, I raced off to the store to buy one of those fans. Next, I had a date with a friend, after which I planned to run to the post office and mail the fan—special delivery. At lunch, I told my friend about my errand, and she laughed so hard the tears fell on her tuna salad. 'Give me the fan,' she said. 'I am going to give it to my daughter.' I was outraged! Why should I give her child my child's fan? My child needs it! My friend asked, 'Did your daughter write and ask you for a fan?' I had to confess that she had not. Come to think of it, she hadn't even mentioned the heat in her letters.

" 'Well,' my friend continued, 'my daughter *asked* me to get her a fan today. And I am going to give her that gift, your fan. You are going to give your daughter an even bigger gift, two weeks in which she manages her life without any unasked-for assistance from you. It's an expensive gift for you to give her. Staying out of her life for two weeks will cost you a lot. But let her sweat . . . or figure out what she needs and ask for it, from you or from someone else.'

"And so ends the story of how my friend's daughter got a fan, how I got to worry about the heat for another week, and how my daughter and I got to separate—just a bit."

My colleague Devora chose to have a bone-marrow transplant as part of her fight against cancer. The treatment involved a monthlong physical separation from her four children, ages two through ten. I asked her how she dealt with this. "I was helpless to change the reality that we would be apart, so in the weeks before I left I focused on the things I could affect. I arranged for a video phone for my home and hospital room. I also consulted a child psychologist for ideas. He suggested that I bring a pad of paper and markers to the hospital so that every day when my husband Mordechai came home from visiting me, he could bring a letter for the children. I made many audiocassettes of stories for the children to listen to while I was gone. Friends who were in theater created a videotape of me with the kids. All these arrangements were a wonderful distraction.

"But what really helped the most was my recognition that my children would be OK without me. I had already had lots of practice in trusting others to take care of my children and in trusting my children to take care of themselves. During the four months before the transplant, I was undergoing such intense chemotherapy that for two weeks out of each month I had to remain in bed. I would hear my two-year-old cry in the next room and know I couldn't lift my head off the pillow. I could also hear someone else going to her and knew that she was fine. One day she was in bed with me, and she was a little cranky. I thought, What should I do to entertain her? Should I sing 'This Little Piggy Went to Market' or should I do 'Humpty-Dumpty'? But the truth was, I was too weak to do anything. So she just looked at me for a long while and then ran off happily to play. I didn't need to *do* anything.

"We feel so responsible to do everything right for our children, but I learned a lot during those months I was sick. We do not always have to make something happen for our kids. When I was in the hospital, my ten-year-old would call and talk and talk and talk. She would share her problems with me. I was too sick to respond, but that was fine. It turned out she could figure out a lot of her issues for herself. What she needed was a loving presence."

There is risk involved in trusting our children to get along without us, in trusting the universe enough to let them go. Kris had the faith to do that, and his child benefited. Kris and his wife, Brenda, already had a bright and healthy three-year-old daughter when they decided to adopt their second child. In those days there was a surplus of babies and a shortage of good homes. They got Eric from a small fishing village in western Canada when he was an infant. Although Eric had learning disabilities, Kris and Brenda faced the challenges matter-of-factly, engaging tutors and special schools and delighting in the ways in which he outshone the other three members of the family. Eric was the only one of the four who intuitively knew how to fix a television set or catch a fish.

When Eric was twelve, Kris and his son were watching a TV show about relatives being reunited after a war. Kris watched Eric carefully for his response. When it was over, Kris turned to him. "Are you thinking about your mother?" he asked. Eric acknowledged that he was. They had planned to explore contact with Eric's "other mother" (as Brenda and Kris referred to her) when Eric was eighteen. But now it seemed the time was right. Kris and Brenda decided to take a risk. They were apprehensive, but they trusted their love for their son and his love for them. Kris wrote to the village and within a short time heard from Eric's biological mother, who indeed was happy to make contact. Kris and his wife spoke to the woman several times and finally decided to let their son speak to her. After several phone conversations, the mother invited Eric for a visit.

Kris and Brenda wanted desperately to keep their son home. What if his other mother tried to keep him in the village? Worse, what if he wanted to stay? But they also knew that they needed to have faith. After many hours of discussion (and several phone calls to a couple they knew who lived in the same village as the mother), they decided to let him go.

He arrived to a wonderful welcome-home party attended by the whole village. They even had a cake decorated with "Welcome Home, Eric." He learned his birth name, Jimmy Barnes. He also discovered that in his native culture, the skill that was most necessary and respected was—fishing! Two weeks later, he returned home glowing and content, knowing that his other mother was safe and well fed (he had always worried she was hungry and had learned that she had a freezer full of elk meat). He told Kris and Brenda, "I used to be Jimmy Barnes, but now I'm Eric Kline." Now he really knew who he was.

Says Kris, "Looking back, I think it was a little crazy. We never spoke to him on the phone during his visit. It was possible that he would not have been able to handle this without us. But this was not something we could handle *for* him in any event. If someone asked me my advice in such a situation, I would have advised against it. We took a risk that was not rational. But isn't having children a remarkable gamble anyway? We did it on faith, and it turned out to be a good thing to do. I never felt like either of my children really belonged to me. With an adopted child, that was even clearer. Eric also belonged to this woman who gave life to him, and he belonged to the universe, and to himself. I had to let him find out who he really was."

The core spiritual truth of parenting is that we do not create our children, nor do we have them forever. The foster parent knows most poignantly what it takes the rest of us a long time to understand: *our children are on loan.* To learn more about this truth, I interviewed a foster mother. Donna was a successful social worker specializing in troubled adolescents. Because she was unable to conceive her own child with her husband, Stan, Donna and Stan decided to become foster parents. Geena, an eight-year-old girl living with an emotionally disturbed abusive mother, needed a home immediately, and Donna and Stan were told that they could probably adopt her in a few years.

Geena arrived with just a few tattered clothes (when she had received a piece of jewelry from a relative, her mom had taken it for herself), a taste for sausages (Donna and her husband ate vegetarian health foods), and a bottomless desire for love. The first day she arrived, she asked Donna, "Do you love me?" Donna did not, of course, love her yet. She had barely met her. But when she said "Yes," that was all Geena needed to hear.

Geena was a high-spirited, fun child, and soon Donna was in love for real. They sewed, they did art projects, they baked, they played dress-up, they read stories. Donna gave Geena constancy, love, and a new world in which a mother did more than smoke cigarettes and watch TV all day. In return, Geena gave Donna the world of childhood.

Even with the abuse she had suffered, Geena still possessed a magical childlike core that was unharmed. Once when it started to rain, Geena asked, "Can I go outside and play in the rain?" Donna, eager to be a responsible mother, said, "No!" But when she could not think of a good reason for the prohibition, she put on her raincoat and joined Geena outside.

After three years, Geena was thriving. Then the phone call came. Geena's father, who had left her mother a few weeks after Geena was born, was now married with children in California and wanted Geena back. Geena had to face the challenge of moving to a strange state to live with a parent and a stepfamily she had never met. Both she and Donna cried for days, but there was nothing to be done. Her father had the legal right to his daughter; Donna did not.

So Donna and Stan drove Geena to the airport with promises that when she was eighteen she could come back and be their daughter in whatever way she wanted. As painful as it was to separate, Donna now says, "I feel good about what I did with Geena. I didn't create her, and by the time I got her, there was already a lot of baggage. I did the absolute best I could and learned a great deal about myself in the process. I got to play in the rain. Now she's gone and I miss her terribly. But to me the whole experience was a gift."

None of us really possesses our children, and almost all of them eventually leave us. If, like Donna, we do the best we can, learn what there is to learn, and are grateful for the gift—whatever the length—we can rejoice. In the end, what remains is the bond of love. Several parents I talked with recalled a children's book, *The Runaway Bunny*, in which a small bunny is reassured by his mother that wherever he goes, she will follow. If he ends up in the sea, she will become a fisherman; if he ends up as a mountain climber, she will become a mountain. The illustrations portray the mother bunny transformed into the different shapes of the things she will become. Some think it is a horrible image: a mother who would never let go, who would spend her life twisting herself out of shape to become whatever it was the child was involved in.

Others, however, find the book comforting, and so do their children. (It has been a best-seller in the children's market since it was published more than fifty years ago.) What the book really says, one mother interpreted, is that in every new place your child goes, she will find your love, transformed into a new shape.

This was certainly the message of a Catholic church retreat weekend Nicole participated in just before she graduated from high school. As she described it, by that point she was sure that religion was one of the things she was leaving behind when she left for college. She was not eager to attend the weekend. Finally, when her father bribed her with the promise of a hundred dollars on her return, she went.

Those two and a half days in the parochial school gym changed her life. The theme of the weekend was "What is love?" The teens shared long, intense discussions about their feelings toward their families, toward other people. How do you experience love? How do you give it? They did lots of singing and prayer services. They lit many, many candles. Nicole realized during the weekend that she was actually terrified about her upcoming separation from her large and loving family.

On Saturday afternoon, the participants were driven to a home for severely disabled children, and each teenager played with a particular child for several hours. Sunday morning, when emotions were high, the climactic moment arrived. Each participant was handed a set of letters (collected by the organizers in advance) written by her mother, her father, and each of her siblings. The letters were about how much she was loved. There were many tears, many prayers, and more candles.

When it was all over, Nicole refused to take the hundred dollars from her father. She felt she had already been given the most valuable gift possible. The weekend "allowed me to leave home feeling that I was enveloped in love, and forever after I associated that love with God and spirituality," she said. "Whenever I needed it, I could access those feelings of love by going to church." Nicole never lost the sense that separation from those she loved, while inevitable, was only physical.

The challenge for parents is to believe that when our children are gone from us, we are still in some sense connected. When my children were small, I taught them a poem to say at night when we were apart:

> *I see the moon*
> *And the moon sees me*
> *And the moon sees someone I want to see*
> *God bless the moon*
> *And God bless me*
> *And God bless someone I want to see.*

When we are well connected, we can tolerate separation. Dr. Weinraub, the expert in (other people's) separation, told me, "I used to observe mothers as they watched their children through the one-way mirror after they had left the children in day care. The mothers would often seem surprised at how happy the children were, and sometimes even a little put off, as if to say, 'If he really loved me, he'd miss me more.' I would assure them, quite truthfully, that just the opposite was the case. Well-loved, well-bonded children show far *less* distress when separating than do those with a tenuous hold on their parents to begin with. We know this already from grief research. The worst grieving is always when the relationship is most ambivalent. People whose love is clean suffer when they lose their loved ones, but they move on."

We will never be fully apart. Whether through our mutual faith in God or a mutual devotion to watching the moon, our sturdy bonds of connection with each other allow us to separate and yet not separate, to stretch like a rubber band and not break. If the small separations are made harder by the knowledge of the great ones to come, perhaps they can also be eased by remembering they are part of a larger plan in which, as the folk saying goes, "We are the archer, and they are the arrow."

The hardest separations are when the arrow does not fly in the direction the parent aimed. Sometimes we parents must be prepared to give up our centrality in our children's lives. Joe, a brilliant professor of mathematics, told me one of the most difficult stories of all. Joe's oldest child, the son on whom he showered "unconditional love," never found his place in their upper-middle-class world. He had learning disabilities that were not diagnosed at the time and other problems that followed in their wake. Eventually he dropped out of high school and hung around the house, depressed, until Joe knew he had to act. "He would be there still," says Joe, "but we gave him a choice: therapy, schooling, a job, or leave."

Joe's son chose the last option. When their friends were driving their children to Harvard or Yale, Joe and his wife drove their son to the local YMCA. Eventually, their son found his way to the army. Over the years, he became a successful career officer, grew in confidence, and is now happily married. Joe, a long-standing peace activist who still wears a ponytail, found himself sitting in the bleachers at one of his son's army events thinking, "Whoever said God doesn't have a sense of humor?"

Although Joe sees his son occasionally and receives a call on birthdays and holidays, the truth is that father and son do not have much in common. Joe would prefer a son whose values, interests, and lifestyle more closely matched his own; more important, Joe would love to be able to connect emotionally with his child. Nevertheless, Joe is gratified that his son has found a life that works for him. "We gave him his life, and he took it.

"For me," Joe reflects, "love is letting people be who they are. I can exist with my son on the terms he wants. I don't have to have it my own way. My well-being doesn't depend on this relationship being as I would like it." He thought about it for a long time. "Perhaps *this* is unconditional love."

My sister, a psychologist, pointed out that this chapter has been a highly personal treatment of the subject of separation, reflecting my own bias. I recognize that the way I approached this topic has a great deal to do with my gender, my ethnicity, my own psychological makeup. This issue is so close to my core that I noticed I was even having trouble "separating" from the topic—that is, finishing the chapter.

I decided to go back and interview Devora again.

"Did you ever consider not doing it?" I asked Devora about her long separation from her children during her hospital stay.

"Not even for two seconds," she replied. "The core of my treatment plan was based on the desire not to be prematurely separated from my children by death. My greatest fear, in the beginning of my illness, was that I might die so soon that my two younger children would not remember me. I believed this treatment would lengthen my life. So I had no ambivalence."

"How did this change you as a parent?"

"When I began, I managed my feelings by focusing on my goal of *not* separating by death. I worked on concrete ways to remain connected. But ultimately I needed to completely surrender *all* my ambitions. By the end, I could honestly say it didn't matter if the little ones remembered me or not. The goal of parenting is not for them to remember us. Parenting is not about our egos; it is *about* separating."

I had thought that the spiritual issue in separation was trust—trusting others with our children, trusting our children with their lives. I had also seen a spiritual theme in the ways we stay connected even when we are physically apart: what matters most is invisible to the eye. But perhaps the most profound spiritual issue in separation, as in life, is surrender.

We make the journey with our children for as long as we can. We cannot, however, control our place in their imagination. All we can do is treasure their place in ours and, beginning with the first baby-sitter's visit, practice letting go.

Chapter 15

MIDNIGHT

Pain

*"There is just one thing I do not understand
about all this death and stuff:* why?"

Centuries ago a saint called his moments of deepest suffering and doubt the "dark night of the soul." F. Scott Fitzgerald agreed and went on to say that in the most desolate part of us it is *always* three o'clock in the morning. Many of us associate the middle of the night with emergencies, with loneliness, with illness and death. When life is hard, nights are the hardest part. Some of my worst memories recall the middle of a night: lying in a hospital in premature labor, waking my daughter every two hours to assess the effects of a concussion earlier that day, sitting sleepless upstairs while my mother-in-law was dying in the living room below.

At midnight, in the dark, the questions are always the same. They begin with the word "why?" Children ask the same questions during the day. Adults who have been hurt by life can bind up their wounds by being cynical or keeping busy. Children tear off the bandages and expose the still-bleeding spots. Children want to know why their dog died, why God created deer ticks, why Jews were sent to the gas chambers, why kids get shot in our cities, why we are destroying the ozone layer.

The truth is, we do not know.

Recently, I conducted a service project at my children's school in which we visited a nursing home weekly over a period of several months. I began by meeting with the children and asking them about their expectations. What were their hopes? Their fears? One of the children volunteered, "I did this project with you last year, and when we came for the last session, the lady who was my buddy had died." This precipitated a long discussion in which the children shared their own experiences with death—pets, grandparents, neighbors, and a friend from the school who had died earlier that year from leukemia.

After many tears and much hand-holding around the table, it was time for the children to go back to their classrooms. As they filed out, one little boy with huge blue eyes came up to me and said, "Can I ask you one question?" I nodded. "There's just one thing I still don't understand about all this death and stuff: *why?*" What Aaron was asking about was loss, the losses Annie Dillard calls "the extraordinary rent you have to pay" to be a resident of this earth.

I told him that if I could answer his question, I would be on *Oprah* that very afternoon and everyone in the whole world would want to watch me. Each of the great religions I have studied has been concerned, if not obsessed, with the question of human pain. Siddhartha Gautama, who later became the Buddha, began his spiritual search precisely because he discovered, to his shock and dismay, that outside the walls of the palace in which he had been raised lay suffering, sadness, loss, and, at the end of life, extinction. The Psalms, which formed the nucleus of ancient Israelite prayer, are filled with cries of despair and questions: "How long, O God, will you forget me?" "Why do you hide yourself in times of trouble?" At the core of Christianity, Jesus on the cross is scorned by society, abandoned by his friends, and left to die a brutal death, believing God has abandoned him. A God who would achieve solidarity with men and women must suffer real pain. How else could God know us and truly be with us?

Yet not one of these religions, nor any other, has come up with a really satisfactory answer to Aaron's question, "Why?" The great religious traditions, at their base, scorn theological speculation. In the Book of Job, three friends come to comfort Job with theology. At the end, God appears to say their efforts were misguided. God says, in so many words, that if Job is looking for answers, he will have to wait a long time. The only "answer" for Job is simply this: *God shows up.* Life lived in the presence of the holy is a response to suffering.

I learned this lesson over and over from parents as they talked about suffering and their children. None had any answers. But in trying to help their children through pain, loss, and death, parents begin to learn, in Rainer Maria Rilke's words, "to love the questions themselves." Rilke went on to say, "Do not seek the answers which cannot be given you because you would not be able to live them. . . . Live the questions now. Perhaps you will then gradually, without noticing it, live along some distant day into the answer." Parents learned that while they could not answer their children's questions, their children could become their companions as they lived along into the answers.

At the time of our interview, my colleague Mordechai had four children under the age of ten; his wife Devora, whom you met in the last chapter, was struggling with cancer. I asked him how he explained their troubles to his children. He looked surprised, thought a while, and then responded, "They don't ask for explanations.

"Last winter, before Devora got sick, we went through what seemed at the time to be a very difficult period. We had a new baby, our car was stolen, and—just as winter was setting in—there was a fire in our house that necessitated our moving out for one week. In a rented car, we had to set out with some bags of clothes and supplies to live somewhere else. At first some friends put us up, and then our insurance came through for a hotel.

"We didn't present all this to the children as a crisis or a disaster or a horrible problem. We treated it as an adventure. We were going to get to visit three different families in three nights and have school-night sleepovers! And then we got to stay at a hotel with a pool! The kids did fine and returned to their lives none the worse for wear. We learned something important. We had the power to frame the situations in our lives, and as parents we had the power to frame them for the children as well. In fact, that was our duty.

"That September, Devora found out she had cancer. During the months she was so sick from the treatments that she could hardly get out of bed, our kids never asked why this was happening to them. That just wasn't the question. *We* never asked why this was happening to them. We never gave the kids the message that their mother's illness was a terrible tragedy that had to be explained. Nor did we treat it as a radical break in their lives. We did not pretend it was something good. But we helped them conceptualize the issue. As parents, our job is not so much to answer questions as to model how to deal with adversity."

I admired Mordechai's explanation but remained a bit incredulous. I could see where late nights with friends and swimming pools might be an adventure, but where was the adventure in having a mother who had to miss your birthday party because she was throwing up? Mordechai insisted, "It's still up to us to frame it the way we want. For months and months, Devora could not cook dinner. Our friends organized a system so that every day a different person brought a fully cooked dinner in aluminum foil pans and left it on our porch with a note. Every evening, we would look forward to discovering who had brought dinner and what they had brought.

"Sometimes the food was great, and sometimes we would have to laugh at how terrible it was. Once we got four lasagnas in one week! I would point out to the children how lucky we were to have so many different friends bringing us food each night. I helped them realize what amazing lessons about community they were learning from this experience. We can't help what happens to them. But we provide the lenses through which they see their world and make sense of it."

"Childhood," wrote Edna St. Vincent Millay, "is the kingdom where nobody dies. Nobody that matters, that is." Most of us remember when we left that kingdom. What mattered most was how the adults around us understood death. Two mothers shared with me two disparate memories of growing up in two very different families.

"For me," said Ursula, "death was scary and creepy. When I was a little girl, my grandfather died. I was not included in the funeral or anything, but I sensed that dark and foreboding things were going on all around me. After the death, my father inherited his father's gold watch. The first time he wore it, the watch stopped—dead—at exactly the hour my grandfather had died. My father was so freaked out by this that he put the watch in his drawer and never got it fixed. No one ever mentioned my grandfather again. Sometimes I would open the drawer and look at that watch. It was spooky to me."

The other mother, Geraldine, recalling her childhood said, "My father always felt very comfortable with death, and that made me feel comfortable too. He would frequently take us for walks in the cemetery near our home. Most of our ancestors were buried there. Since Dad seemed to like the place so much, it was an outing we all enjoyed. Dad's own father was not buried in that cemetery; he had asked to be cremated. We still had Granddad's ashes on the mantle over the fireplace in our home. Dad had wrapped the box in brightly colored gift paper and set it there years ago, according to his father's final request. Granddad had adored presents! When I brought my fiancé home for the first time at Christmas, we were opening the presents, and he lifted the box and said, 'Who's this for?' We all said, 'Don't worry about that, it's just Granddad.' Joe turned white as a sheet, but we all thought it was very funny."

These examples are extreme; most of us fall somewhere in the middle. But none of us understands death, for none of us really knows what happens after people die. Our children, however, hope that we do. For some parents, it is enough to communicate to children a sense of mystery. Isabella, the mother of two girls, one with cerebral palsy, told me how her children love to watch the cartoon version of *Charlotte's Web* on video. "My handicapped daughter feels especially vulnerable, and she cries and cries every time Charlotte dies. When the videotape is over, my kids always ask a million questions: Where are we going to go when we die? Is it very far away? Will God have a bed for us? I tell them that E. B. White wrote this book to be about the miracle of birth and the miracle of friendship and the miracle of death. (I read somewhere that he said that.) It always stops them short. What do you mean the miracle of death? How is death a miracle? They think I'm saying something strange, but they keep thinking about it. The whole book is about birth and life and nature and death, and it does seem to communicate that the whole package is miraculous."

Particularly in this realm, parents often find that their children are their greatest teachers and spiritual guides. Hannah's children were all in their thirties when her oldest child, her beloved son Mark, died of AIDS. In the weeks before his death, Mark's three sisters devoted themselves to his care. After he died, they gave full reign to their grief. "They adored their brother, and they didn't mind showing their pain—in private, in public, just anywhere. For me, it was an awakening. My own brother had died in a car accident many years before, when I was pregnant with Mark. The first time I ever wore a maternity dress was to my brother's funeral. I had thought it important at the time to maintain equanimity and control, to be strong, to help my parents. Through Mark's death, my daughters taught me by letting loose. They allowed me to grieve for my son and, amazingly, finally grieve for my brother."

Al, whose eight-year-old daughter died in an emergency room surrounded by her brothers and sisters, told me, "The doctor didn't think Sally could hear anything anymore, but we all kept talking to her anyway. At a certain point, her little sister Annie, who was three, stretched out her arm and pointed upward. 'Go, Sal!' she said clearly and firmly, in a voice full of love. There was a look of peace on Annie's face. A minute later the doctor said that Sally had died. We all held on to that image for a very long time."

In Betty's case, she began the work of creating images for her daughter, but her child completed the job. One day, Betty took her three-year-old daughter Gail and Gail's beloved stuffed Giraffe for a walk in the stroller. When they reached their home, they realized that Giraffe was no longer with them. Betty and Gail walked back over the route of the walk, searching everywhere for Giraffe. Gail began to cry, even as she kept talking about finding Giraffe someday.

As they walked back home, they passed an open manhole in the street. "Maybe Giraffe fell down there," Betty suggested. Gail began to weep. On one level, the image of the manhole had worked. It had helped Gail understand that this loss was final, that she would not see Giraffe again. On another level, though, the picture of the event that it offered—Giraffe lying in a dark hole, deep below the street—was simply unacceptable to Gail.

Betty had gotten across the permanence of death, but Gail needed something more. A few minutes later, Gail's face brightened. "I know what happened, Mommy! After I dropped Giraffe, a nice man saw him lying there and took him home to his daughter who needed a toy. The man and his daughter are taking good care of Giraffe now." Betty was stunned. How could she have needed a three-year-old to help her see the obvious? Giraffe was gone, but there still could be sense to the loss. Gail had accepted the permanence of the loss to her but had needed a story that gave her tragedy meaning from a larger perspective. So she created one. "A nice man, indeed," Betty mused, her eyes welling up with tears as she told me the story.

Ellen, a liberal Jew, reported another lost-toy story. In the Jewish liturgy, there is a blessing in which God is praised for bringing the dead back to life. It was written at a time when, unlike today, the resurrection of the body was a firmly held belief in Judaism. In addition to saying the blessing daily as part of the standard morning, afternoon, and evening prayers, a traditional Jew will say the blessing when encountering a friend whom he has not seen in a very long time. Liberal Jewish prayer books typically rewrite the blessing to say, "God gives life to all things." As for Ellen, she was sure it was all an ancient belief and not part of anything she had experienced or ever would.

Then something happened to change her mind.

"Our last night on a trip to Europe we were in Zurich. We stayed in a huge, impersonal airport hotel because we had to take an early plane home the next morning. In the rush of departure, our daughter left behind the beloved teddy bear she had slept with every night since she was two. The first two weeks back in Baltimore she was grief stricken. We purchased an identical bear at the store, but being brand new, he did not look or feel or smell the same.

"One day, I returned home from work to find a misshapen package on our doorstep with the mail. By the grace of the efficient innkeeping of the Swiss, the bear had returned. To my utter surprise, I found my mouth opening, and I heard myself saying out loud, 'Praised are you who brings the dead back to life.' And then I found myself thinking, 'This is the part we never get to see.'

"I wept tears of joy. Ever since I became a mother, I had wanted my child to believe that the unbelievable might sometimes occur, that magic could happen. And now it had, in her life. But the truth was, I had really wanted to believe in magic myself. As it turns out, she was much less amazed by this whole event than I. She simply did not realize how unlikely it was for a big establishment to go out of its way for a child."

A belief once relegated to metaphor in Ellen's modern mind had leaped into the realm of the possible. "I kept thinking to myself—it *is* possible. You could love something. You could lose it in a way that you were certain you would never see it again. And you could see it again! *Why not?* I am sure I do not know how or where or in what form God gives us life after we are dead, but I am sure it is possible."

In the confusion of pain and loss, some parents discover a role for ritual. When I teach theology to rabbinical students, I love to include a piece from a journalist's collection of interviews. This particular interview is with a young mother whose son died after a long and terrible illness. In the midst of the illness, she met a rabbi at a party. "Over the cheese dip," she asked him for guidance, although she was not Jewish. She asked the rabbi why all this horror had befallen her family. He replied that he hadn't the slightest idea. But he did have a crazy thought. He suggested that on Friday night she clear all the pill bottles off the table, put on a white tablecloth, have everyone sit down at the same time, and eat a nice dinner. That was it. No prayers, just an island of beauty in the midst of the chaos in the home.

She followed his advice and grew to love their variation on Jewish Sabbath observance. But this story isn't about Judaism at all. Any religion would have done the trick. This mother needed something outside herself to help her transcend her situation. The rules of Sabbath are arbitrary. But they work. Recipes for behavior are not answers, but they fill the void. And they point beyond it.

Sometimes parents are driven to invent ritual to help their children through unprecedented situations. When a plane crash killed two children in a school playground near our home, the many surviving children who were present for the event were devastated. The school handled both the physical and, to some extent, the psychological fallout with great professionalism. Being a public institution, it had less confidence addressing the spiritual dimension.

Carl decided to fill the gap for his son. He made a scrapbook of clippings from the numerous articles that filled the newspapers for days after the event. Each year on the anniversary of the crash, he sits down with his son and reads the scrapbook with him. Then they walk over to the school yard and put flowers at the spots where the two children were killed. Said Carl, "I don't believe children forget this kind of thing. The school culture has not yet found a place to honor that memory year after year, but we can do it in our family." By addressing something terrifying and abnormal in a routinized and caring way, we try to point beyond the chaos to the order, beyond the harshness to what is gentle in the universe.

There are other pointers. In Ruth's case, it was not ritual but superstition that helped her transcend a legacy of suffering and death. Ruth grew up among Orthodox Jews, all survivors of the Holocaust. Her own parents had each lost their entire families, including their respective spouses and children, in the camps. After the war, her parents had met, married, come to America, and had Ruth. She grew up with a huge pall of suffering hanging over her life. "In the midst of every celebration, there was always the knife." There was a box of photographs of her half brothers and sisters, but no one ever looked at them. Ruth's parents' response to their suffering was a firmer resolve to follow God's law as strictly as possible.

Yet Ruth simply glowed with spiritual energy. I asked her how she had developed into such a strong, confident, joyous person despite her parents' past. Ruth thought about it for a long time. "My best friend was also the child of two survivors. Her mother was a deeply religious person from Eastern Europe. She was like a second mother to me. She would sit for hours telling my friend and me stories of Poland before the war, colorful stories of simple people with strong beliefs in goblins. Stories about the goblins. It was a strength to be touched by such stories.

"My friend's mother would often look at my palm and point out a certain vein in it and say, 'That vein shows that you are destined for greatness, destined for beauty, for love, for great joy.' I believed her totally, and it happened just as she predicted, because I believed it." The world of myth she inherited from her second mother helped Ruth to build a new vision of herself in the midst of her parents' pain.

Although parents have no answers for their children's sorrow, compassion, if not an answer, is at least a response. Lewis told me about his son. "When Bernie was seven, there was a boy in his class named Jimmy who needed a heart transplant. The class did a walkathon for the kid, and they all felt great about it. Then, just before the transplant was going to occur, Jimmy died. Bernie wasn't sleeping well. For several weeks, he'd wake up over and over during the night. He kept saying, 'Why would a kid die?'

"I suggested he write a letter to the family telling them what their son meant to him. He did. He was distressed when no answer arrived. I explained that he might never hear from the family but that it would mean a great deal to them that he had written. A few weeks later, a woman I had never met came up to me at the swimming pool and said that she wanted to meet my son. She knelt to his level and said, 'I want to thank you for the letter you sent us. It was important for us to know that Jimmy is still alive in your heart.' That night Bernie slept soundly for the first time."

When Claudia's children were eight and five, she was bedridden by a childhood hip problem that had recurred. Two years of excruciating pain followed, along with the inability to do even simple tasks. During that period, she had four surgeries, only the last of which helped—and then only partially. Throughout those years, her husband would leave for work at 6:00 A.M. so that he could get home in time to make dinner. "Every morning for two years my older son had to put on my socks and shoes. It was either that or I'd go barefoot all day. Every morning. Maybe six hundred times.

"As for my younger son, when I got depressed and was in too much pain to do anything but lie in bed, he would come and lie down next to me and just hold me. Later, when I walked with a cane, my sons would walk with me and let me lean on them. They became nurturing, caring people.

They had to change the linens on their own beds every week, and neither one could do it alone. So they had to do it together. Now they are each other's best friends. I do not believe that pain is good. But when I look at my children, I think that my life has been good, and I would not wish away the parts that have been hard."

Seth remembers that when he was a little boy, whenever things were difficult for him, his father would tell him a story. Once, King Solomon was given a gift. It was a ring whose message was so wise that it could be applied to any occasion. It was the perfect message for a day of great joy as well as one of great sorrow. The message: This too shall pass.

"As a child, I did not understand or appreciate this story," Seth recalls. "It did not help me one bit in a situation of pain. Children, after all, live in the present."

I asked Seth why he was telling me about this story if it was so unsuccessful.

"Because now I tell the story to our children. They don't seem to find it any more meaningful than I did at their age. But now, *I* find it helpful."

"The world is like a wedding hall," the Talmud says. A rather improbable remark, given all the pain. *How is it like a wedding hall?* A nineteenth-century Hasidic rabbi tried to explain the Talmudic adage with a story. A man came to a town and heard singing and dancing from a particular building. He asked what was going on and was told it was a wedding. The next night the same thing happened. And the night after that. Finally, the man questioned how one family could have so many weddings. "That is not a home!" he was told. "It is a wedding hall. Tonight one couple is getting married there, tomorrow someone else."

And so, too, the world. There is always some joy, some celebration, some wedding in process, but it is not always the same person's wedding. You are not always the one at the party. And sometimes the hall is closed for the night.

The music always fades, the hall is ultimately darkened and a lock put on the door after midnight. But the hall inevitably opens the next morning. The lights are turned back on, and the instruments retuned. Our thoughts turn toward morning, toward the future, toward hope.

Chapter 16

FOUR A.M.

Hope

Weeping may tarry for the night
But joy comes in the morning.
PSALM 30

It was 4:00 A.M. The house was dark, quiet. Gina had been pacing the floor all night with her four-year-old son, Jim, in her arms. Jim tended to run high fevers, but this night had been exceptional, even for him. Every hour, it seemed, his fever shot up another degree. When the thermometer registered 105, Gina called the doctor. "Take his temperature again in ten minutes," he directed. "If it continues going up, meet me at the emergency room." As she began to watch the clock, Gina felt herself shaking. Could her son die? Seven minutes passed, eight minutes. Then, without warning, Jim's fever broke. He started to sweat profusely, his temperature began to drop, and his eyes came into focus. A few minutes later, light appeared in the sky.

It is hell to live without hope. Mordecai Kaplan observed that it is in this sense, if no other, that religion saves men and women from hell. During one of the darkest periods of Jewish history, the Roman occupation of Palestine, hope for victory over our enemies or improvement of our material lot seemed most unlikely. It was then that the Jewish people began to believe fervently in the promise of a divinely sent redeemer, a "Messiah" who would miraculously usher in the kingdom of God on earth. This faith gave Jews (and later Christians who believed the process had been inaugurated through Jesus) access to great expectation, great belief in the future. The notion of the Messiah has helped both Jews and Christians trust in the ultimate victory of good, and on a day-to-day level, it has provided the optimism that allows us to move forward toward possibilities. Theologians call it redemption; regular people speak about hope.

What does all this have to do with children? Tradition has it that Elijah, the prophet who will announce the Messiah's arrival, makes an appearance at every Jewish birth ceremony. Does that mean that each baby might be the Messiah? Perhaps. Does it mean, as the Irish folk saying proclaims, that every new baby is a sign that God has not given up on us yet? As Carl Sandburg said, "A baby is God's opinion that life should go on." The final redemption clearly has not yet come; there is still healing needed. And so a new generation must be born.

Many parents see their choosing to have a child as a kind of affirmation of hope, a statement that it is all worth it somehow. However difficult they have found life to be, they have made the choice to go ahead and create more life, believing that it is worth the struggle. The novelist Anne Lamott pondered the agonizing issue of "how on earth anyone can bring a child into this world knowing full well that he or she is eventually going to have to go through seventh and eighth grades."

On a more serious note, one of the highest birthrates in the world was found in displaced-person camps after World War II. Paradoxically, people responded to utter chaos and destruction by having children. John, an antinuclear activist, told me, "At the time I decided to have a child, I believed on an intellectual level that it was likely we would have a nuclear war. Yet on some deeper level, I guess I had confidence that we would not, because I helped create another generation. Doing so strengthened my faith in the future. I would look out at the world through my child's eyes, and the future seemed longer. It was like placing a bet on a horse and then growing surer that the horse would win."

How do children provide hope? A story in the Talmud suggests one possibility. Once, while Rabbi Akiva was walking in a cemetery, he met a man who was carrying a heavy load of wood on his back. Akiva learned that the man was dead and was being punished for having been a sinner in his life. Each day he was forced to carry wood for a fire that was then used to burn his body. Akiva further discovered that at the time of the man's death, his wife had been pregnant. If Akiva could find the man's child and teach him to stand up in synagogue and lead the community in prayer, the father would be redeemed and released from his suffering.

Akiva found the family, painstakingly taught the man's son the Hebrew alphabet, and eventually the boy stood in synagogue to say the appropriate words. At that moment, the father was released from his retribution. He appeared to Akiva in a dream and thanked him, for now he was free. The tradition adds, "The protection children provide for their parents is greater than the protection parents provide for their children. Parents can only protect their children in this world (and even then, only sometimes). But children, by good deeds, can protect their parents from retribution in the world to come."

But can they? Appealing as this fable may be, I believe it is just that—a fable. We cannot look to our children to make up for our failings, to provide us recompense for our sufferings, to give our lives an integrity they otherwise lack. Our failures remain failures, whether we have ten children or none. A son cannot take a father out of hell, except in Talmudic tales.

Recently, however, I conducted a funeral that reminded me of that story about Akiva. A woman called the rabbinical college where I teach. She wanted a rabbi to do a funeral service for her mother, Ilsa, who had just died at age eighty-three. Ilsa had not lived as a Jew her entire adult life, nor had she raised her children as Jews. She had hidden her Jewish identity from everyone, including her children. It was only when they were grown that her children had learned their mother's story.

The daughter told me the little she knew. Ilsa was born a Jew in Berlin. In the early 1930s she was a medical student. One night, the president of the university called her to his office. He handed her a forged passport and told her to take the next train out of Germany. "Don't call home, don't discuss this with anyone. Don't even go back to your room to pack." She did as she was told. Just before the train crossed over the Swiss border, Nazi soldiers came through and took everyone with a Jewish passport off the train. While she watched from the window, they were all shot. She proceeded on to America, determined not to have anything more to do with the identity that seemed to bring nothing but trouble. She would not pass that burden on to the next generation.

Ilsa's children learned their mother's story when, in order to be the mother she wanted to be, she needed to share it. Shortly after being discharged from military service in Vietnam, Ilsa's son learned that his entire unit had been blown up. His life fell apart. To help him heal, Ilsa shared her own story of survival.

Having heard the whole saga, the children were saddened by their mother's sense that she needed to live a lie, even so many years later. Ilsa's daughter understood and empathized for she, too, had lived "in the closet" as a lesbian for many years. When Ilsa died, her son, her daughter, and her daughter's lover made one clear decision: "Mother does not have to hide anymore."

After eulogizing Ilsa, I intoned the traditional Hebrew prayers that would have been familiar to this woman's ancestors but that were totally foreign to her children. On the children's behalf, I said Kaddish, the traditional mourner's prayer, as they sat in polite silence, bewildered by the foreign language and strange tunes.

When it was over, the children offered to make a contribution in their mother's honor to some charity of my choice. I insisted that they choose. They, in turn, decided that the most appropriate recipient would be a synagogue. Because of her trauma and fears, Ilsa had abandoned her identity. But her children did not allow the story to end there. They created out of the occasion of her funeral an opportunity for her to return to her origins.

These children helped repair the brokenness in their mother's life. They made sure that their mother, who had to live a lie, at least could have an honest funeral. And more important, they lifted up the piece of her story that was truly noble and inspiring, the way that she gave up her own silence when she believed it would help her son. Because her children live on to tell that story, Ilsa's courage and compassion as a mother also live on to inspire others.

My children inform me that in the film *The Lion King*, Simba is told that his dead father is alive. He is then led to a pool of water where he gazes at his own reflection, realizing at that moment that his father is alive in him. As parents, many of us take hope from that image and from the knowledge that our children continue our lives and the lives of our ancestors. I remember, for example, the December morning thirteen years ago when we got a call that Seth's grandmother had died. Although I was nine months pregnant, the doctor assured us that Seth had time to make it to the funeral in Pittsburgh. He quickly set out for the Philadelphia airport, but on arrival found that his plane had been canceled. Since the next plane would get him there too late for the funeral, he took a taxi home, arriving just hours before the birth of our first child. "I always felt that the souls of my grandmother and daughter passed in transit," Seth recalls. "I could imagine them waving to each other in the night as one left this earth and one arrived."

But flashes of immortality are only part of the story. I have talked not only to parents whose children have fulfilled their every dream but also to a mother from Italy whose two sons are both in prison on drug charges and a father from Israel who has outlived all three of his children.

Even if they do not carry our lives forward, our children can teach us about hope by demanding of us that we create our own hope. Sometimes, just because of the challenges they provide, just because we realize they cannot redeem us, we grow as human beings. A great Hasidic rabbi, Nachman of Bratslav, hoped that his infant son, for whom he had prayed for many years, was not only *his* redemption but also part of God's plan to redeem the world. Nachman believed that his son might well be the Messiah, or the one from whom the Messiah would come.

But at the age of one and a half, Nachman's son died. After that, says his biographer Arthur Green, Nachman became convinced that "the world was not ready for redemption." Until his own death four years later, Nachman began to write fantastical tales, in order, says Green, to "capture people's hearts with holy fantasies, to prepare their imaginations for belief." Perhaps, too, Nachman needed to heal his *own* imagination. His son, as it turned out, would save neither the world nor his own father from the pain of life. Nachman needed to create other answers for the world and for himself.

For Claudia, who had always found hope and redemption through creativity, motherhood offered yet another, surprising outlet. "I tried many forms of creative expression in my life, but my two greatest loves were dancing and painting. When my child was born, both of those paths were closed to me. It took so long to get the paints set up, and then Nathan would get into them and make a mess. I had no time or space for dancing. I searched for some way to grapple with my experience and create beauty out of it, some way that was more practical under the circumstances. Finally, I hit upon poetry.

"I had never been a poet. But it was perfect. Poetry is an incredibly condensed form; it is all about capturing an essence. And the equipment was ready at hand: I was surrounded in my house by books of poetry and by notebooks and pens. Sometimes I would think of a line for a poem while I was pushing Nathan in the stroller in the woods. When I got back to the car, I'd grab the notebook in the glove compartment and write it down. Then I would twist it in my mind while I was changing his diaper. I believe that in each moment there is the kernel of a poem waiting to be written.

"Whenever I felt depleted and lost, I would try to honor the moment by writing a poem. It would be like taking a journey closer to my core. It anchored me. I was rediscovering life, and this was a way to hold on to my experience. It allowed me to really be in my life and declare its value. I would scribble half-written poems all day amidst the Cheerios. I don't think I ever finished one poem during those years, but having an artistic outlet while my child was young and I was feeling lonely and frustrated sustained me. I was far from the wellsprings that nourished me. I needed a miracle to renew me. Reading and writing poetry were that miracle. I guess all those years my poems were my prayers."

Nachman wrote stories, Claudia poems.

While we might hope that our children will create prayers or stories from our lives when we are gone, our wisest course is to follow Claudia's and Nachman's response. If we do not want to buckle under our own burdens, we cannot afford to count on our children's prayers. We had best say them for ourselves, create our own significance out of the chaos, tell the best stories we can to leave behind. For life is ultimately a struggle each of us wages against meaninglessness.

Serena had to preserve her hope over a long period of time. "Almost thirty years ago," she began, "I was married to a man from Brazil. It was not a good relationship, and after several false starts, I had the strength to end the marriage. I took my five-year-old son Marco with me, for we were deeply connected to each other. Then, in the middle of the night, my ex-husband came to my apartment, made a huge scene, and took Marco back. At that point I felt that I could not fight anymore. I let Marco stay with his father, believing that when he got older we would find ways to reconnect.

"For several years, Marco did not see me again, although I occasionally saw him from a distance. When Marco was eight, I got a call from his father asking to borrow some money. I asked him to call back in a few days while I thought about it. He never called back. About six months later I learned from a friend that the day after our phone conversation, my ex-husband left for Brazil with my son. Days of frantic phone calls convinced me that I did not have the resources to even find, much less forcibly reclaim, my child.

"Part of me was terrified. Is he alive? Is he all right? Does he wonder where I am? Does he hate me? How will he grow up? But part of me had to carry on, go to work every day. I had to convince myself he was fine, that we would see each other again, if not in this life then the next. I began to do yoga, follow a guru, and get in touch with a spiritual part of me.

"Eventually, I fell in love, married again, and had another child. But I never stopped thinking about Marco. I would remember the wonderful moments when he was a toddler and we would spend long days together, going to the playground, the store. I remembered the way he would gaze with wonder at a flower, how when he first began to walk, he would fall and pick himself up and fall again. Every new stage with my new son would remind me of Marco at that age. Later, when I went to friends' children's high school graduations I would think, Marco would be graduating from high school now.

"The one thing I always did as my commitment to Marco was to keep his father's last name. Each year we paid extra so that I could be listed separately from my husband in the Miami phone book. If Marco ever tried to reconnect, he would be able to locate me. One New Year's Day, twenty-five years after Marco was born, twenty years after I was divorced, and seventeen years since I had seen my son, I decided it was time to give up. It was really a recognition that I would never see Marco again. It was time to let go, to finally make the separation complete. I resolved to call the phone company the next day to have my separate listing discontinued. But in the end, I could not do it.

"One morning that spring, I got a phone call from Marco. Through a series of unlikely events, he had found me. That afternoon, I called the phone company and took the separate listing out of the phone book for good."

Serena affirmed the possibility of connection with her son, even when it seemed the most unlikely of outcomes. Sometimes I think our religious practices are like keeping our names in the phone book, just in case God might try to find us. It seems a long shot, but it is a sign of hope.

When I run out of optimism, I think about Beulah. The child of poor farmers in South Carolina, Beulah moved to Chicago after World War II.

She married a man who had been injured during the war, and he was unable to make a steady income. Beulah went to work in a cigar factory to support them. But when Beulah had their first child, she wanted to stay home with the baby, so she chose to take in foster children—seven sons in all. Then, to further supplement her income, she pushed all the furniture in her living room back against the walls and opened a day-care center in her tiny row house. For fifteen years, she cared for no fewer than twelve children a day, six days a week. At high tide, there could be as many as sixteen children playing in her house. Beulah's home opened for business at 6:00 A.M. For several years, she cared for a child whose mother worked the swing shift and who stayed until midnight.

I could not begin to fathom how Beulah maintained her energy and good cheer during those years of near-constant child care. She described her routine. "After the children left, I would get down on my hands and knees and wash the floor thoroughly. Then I would do my own kids' laundry for several hours. A few times a week I walked to the supermarket."

"Did you ever do anything for yourself?" I wondered.

"Once a week," she recalled with a smile, "during the years when I didn't keep the boy who stayed till midnight, I would take the El and then a bus to a beauty parlor that stayed open very late. I'd have my hair done and get home about one in the morning. By five, I was up cooking for the day. Most of the children needed me to serve them breakfast and lunch. Some were still there for supper."

I asked her if she had any regrets about this period in her life. She had only one. "There was an eighth foster son whom I sent back. I got him when he was six, and he was a troublemaker. He tried to light a fire, and I got scared, so I called the social worker and canceled the arrangement, even though I loved him. Now I wish I had kept him. I *know* I could have turned things around for him. I think about him, and I am sorry that I didn't trust myself."

Those busy years are now over, and Beulah's husband is dead. The children who used the day-care center are grown, but many still stay in touch with "Miss B." The foster sons are also grown and scattered, although they too love their foster mother and stay closely connected to her. Beulah's greatest sorrow is that her own son, a brilliant, promising young student, became schizophrenic in his teens and now lives at home with his mother, unable to care for himself. He is by turns incoherent, abusive, and apathetic, and often spends whole days simply wandering the streets, smoking cigarettes. He will probably be this way for the rest of Beulah's life.

Beulah is no Pollyanna; she confesses that her son's illness has been a great trial, that caring for a mentally ill adult is a daily burden that threatens to break her spirit, even as caring for twelve or more lively children all day strengthened it. Yet Beulah says, despite the drudgery, the terror, the disappointment, even in the midst of her current life, she often feels "joy coming up from deep within me."

Beulah's story is about children and hope, because the joy that comes up in her is the joy that was planted there by the years of raising small children. Beulah, however, when asked where the joy comes from, had not a moment's hesitation or doubt: "It's from God."

"I always told my children," Beulah said, "that you can pray to the Lord for anything you want, any little thing at all. But I always stressed to them that just because you ask the Lord for something does not mean the Lord will give it to you. The only prayer the Lord always answers is for peace. God will always find a way to give you hope."

I believe, as Beulah does, that we eventually come to the limits of our own abilities, the edge of what we can rationally conclude about hope. Then we look to our traditions. They tell us that the final hope rests in knowing that God will redeem us all, in God's own good time.

There is a bit of folklore in Aramaic that is sung at the conclusion of every Passover seder, traditionally during the wee hours of the morning, just before dawn—a song called "Had Gadya." It tells the story of a father who bought a goat for two small coins. In the subsequent verses, the goat is eaten by a cat who, in turn, is bitten by a dog who is hit by a stick that is burned by fire . . . and so on. Finally, when the singers are breathless from repeating so many minitales of disaster, the Angel of Death appears and kills a butcher who slaughtered a cow. The last verse of the song concludes the sorry tale with the promise, stated as if it had already occurred, that the Holy One of Blessing will appear and destroy the Angel of Death. By then, everyone laughs with relief that the song is over.

I had always assumed that this song was an afterthought to the seder, something to amuse the children and provide an outlet for the high spirits induced by the mandatory four cups of wine. But recently I realized the song was actually expressing the essence of the seder—the hope that all our sorrows and strife will be healed someday, that the seemingly endless cycle of conflict will be broken, and that good will finally triumph.

The last verse of "Had Gadya" is the part we have yet to witness. Christians believe that because of Jesus the world is no longer condemned to death, that in Christ's resurrection we have seen the first fruits of the liberation. But only the first fruits. Glimpses. On my good days, I believe that someday the Holy One of Blessing will devour the Angel of Death for the very last time. On bad days, I try at least to remember that other people believe that. Until such a time as it happens, we muddle on, buoyed by hope, for which our children can certainly provide motive, if not evidence.

Sometimes our kids turn to us in despair and, looking at a world of violence, of AIDS, of injustice, of ecological gloom and doom, ask us to tell them why we believed in life enough to pass it on to them. We can tell them the story of the goat, or of Jesus, or whatever stories we can tell with conviction. We can also tell them the ways in which we have found hope through connections with others, through our love for our spouse or partner, through deep friendships, and through our relationship with them. Moments of connection provide hints of redemption. And we can tell them that ultimately the meaning our life has is the meaning we impart to it by our effort to deal with whatever comes our way with grace and compassion.

When we stand before our Maker, a Talmudic saying has it, we will be asked several questions about our behavior on earth, all of them ethical in nature. The last question, however, is different and is perhaps the most difficult to answer. God will ask, Did you keep your eye out for the Messiah? In other words, did you continue to expect redemption? Did you hope? It is the answer to that question that is the most important of all.

Sometimes, at 4:00 A.M., before the fever has broken, hope is all we have. And it can be quite a lot.

During the year I was writing this book, I occasionally found myself at meetings or social events frequented by academics. When I told someone my topic, they would promptly ask, "What are your findings?" I would explain, then, that I didn't have any findings. I was interviewing people who were not intended to be representatives of anything but themselves. Furthermore, I was musing about matters that had no neat answers. After a while, I got tired of my little speech. Maybe I did have a "finding" in there somewhere.

So I went back over my interview transcripts. No question, there were themes that reappeared: the awe at the birth experience, the anger when children fought, the quest for meaning inspired by the passionate questions of a child trying to make sense of the world. But every father had his own story, every mother her own idiosyncratic take on the issues. Finally, I noticed something that might be called a finding. Quite a few parents reported that their children had a favorite place for raising religious questions: riding in the backseat of the car. The frequency was so striking it might even have been statistically significant.

This finding is not likely to revolutionize the field of child development, but it does point to a truth. Children feel safe initiating difficult conversations in the car. They know that even if their parent gets embarrassed, there is no escape. The children know they cannot escape either, and perhaps most important, no one has to look the other in the eye. All of these arrangements facilitate communication.

Spirituality is a private matter, perhaps the most private of all matters, and not easy to talk about in the usual way. My grandparents were Lithuanian Jews, called Litvaks by other Jews. When it came to their relationship with God, it was said, "Litvaks do not kiss and tell." It was true. That didn't mean they didn't talk a lot, but when it came to what mattered most, they expressed themselves without words. Take the white robe called the *kittel*, for example. A traditional Jewish man wears his *kittel* each year on the Day of Atonement, when he leads a seder, and on the day of his wedding. When he dies, the man is buried in that very same robe. Who needs words? Once a year you climb into your coffin clothes to fast and pray for a day. You get married in your shroud. What words could equal that statement about life's seriousness, its unity, its power?

I read a story once that touched me deeply. A young girl told how each year she and her grandmother bake a special bread for Easter. On Good Friday afternoon, in a solemn mood, they knead the dough. Then they place the bread in the oven, and grandmother and granddaughter sit sadly together, thinking about the crucifixion of Christ. Soon, however, the wonderful aroma of the baking bread begins to penetrate the gloom, and their mood lightens. On Sunday morning, the grandmother hands her granddaughter a piece of the bread. As she tastes it, the girl knows in her very bones that "Christ has risen."

This whole book is about daily tasks, about physical acts, about rites and traditions and prayers and metaphors. All of these provide support while we try to connect with a Power that otherwise seems abstract or very far away. Words are awkward, embarrassing, inadequate. In the ordinary and the extraordinary moments of parenting, mothers and fathers experience the reality of the unseen, the God beyond God. The prayers, stories, poetry, and customs of a religious tradition can serve as a language beyond language that allows us to live out our belief in that reality and share it with our children.

The candles, the melodies, and the tales of Judaism connect me with my intuitions about life's meaning and help me recover those intuitions during the dry spells. Over and over during my interviews, I heard parents describe a miraculous loop, a circle of wonder. We settle our child for bed. That is parenting technique. When the child is at peace, we experience our own sense of serenity and of trust. Then we have more to give our children. That is grace. We read our child an ancient story as literacy training, and it becomes a vehicle of transcendence for us. When ritual serves as the outward form of an inner transformation, when it helps us to go down deeper, notice the holy moments in an ordinary hour, live closer to what really matters, then religion is working as it should.

I find this process wonderful, amazing; I choose to construct my life around it. Not everyone does. Cary, a British woman with no religious practice, intrigued me. Out of a hundred interviews, hers was the one I kept returning to, meditating on. Her parenting journey had been harrowing, and she has walked it without religious beliefs or stories or rituals, without many friends or neighbors or relatives, without even a strong marriage.

Her only child was born with familial dysautonomia, a genetic disease in which one's body cannot regulate its temperature properly. Multiple complications result. Cary's son was sick every day of his life. When he died in his early thirties, his mother said, "He never had a good day."

Asked about life with a critically ill child, Cary responded bluntly, "At best, it stinks." Cary shouldered the burden of her son's care virtually alone, physically and emotionally, all the years of his life. Her son could never go to school, make friends, get a job. He just got sicker and sicker. "He never even had a chance at a life." One day, Cary met a woman who said to her, "If I had to take care of a child like yours, I'd pull all my hair out," to which Cary replied, "If I did that, I'd have a sick son and also be bald."

What sustained her? I wondered. What got her up in the morning, kept her balance, gave her a sense that all of this suffering had some meaning? "It *didn't* have any meaning," Cary replied. "If I could have known in advance, as mothers of dysautonomics can today, I would surely have had an abortion." I asked her if she found solace in meeting with other mothers in similar situations. She had not sought such support while her son was alive. Now, she says, she occasionally goes to meetings of women who have lost children, but she finds that many of them are "busy on a spiritual quest, interested in the afterlife or other crazy ideas" for which she has no use. As she sees it, "when you're dead, you're dead."

Cary did well by her son, giving him all the care and love she could muster, fighting for his life with doctors and hospitals and saving him on more than one occasion. "I knew him better than the doctors did, and they grew to trust my intuitions. I never called a false alarm, so they knew they could rely on me when I said something needed immediate attention. I feel good about the way I cared for him."

Cary is a vibrant woman, full of energy and vigor, her vitality undiminished by her trials—indeed, perhaps strengthened. When I asked her about her life today, she told me about her interest in the theater, books, golf, tennis, bridge. "The hours of the day are never long enough," she said. "I always tell my friends that if they find me dead, they can rule out suicide." Where did her strength come from? "I inherited it from my mother" was Cary's reply. "She was a very strong woman who weathered all kinds of tragedy and always had a certain joie de vivre. I guess I am like her. It's innate."

I found all this a mystery. I admired Cary and was inspired by her. I felt a spiritual strength in her that evoked my sense of meaning, of purpose, of wonder. Yet she did not interpret her own journey that way at all. For her, it was all very straightforward, matter-of-fact. I was impressed by Cary's refusal to take what, to her, would be "cozy comfort" from ideas of the afterlife. There was something courageous about her choice to live without illusions. I was in awe of her ability to endure great difficulties without any overall sense of meaning.

As I read and reread my interview with Cary, I wrestled with the temptation to make her over in my own image. I wanted her to be religious, even if she did not think she was. I wanted to find out the unconscious depths that really were her spiritual core. I sensed them in her humor. Humor is a powerful religious tool. When we laugh at ourselves, it means we are aware of our frailty, our lack of ultimacy. We acknowledge something that is larger than ourselves. Surely Cary could not have done what she did or continue to be who she is without laughter, without her cynical, biting, but finally saving wit.

But the bottom line is that Cary's story is her own. It is the story of nobility and bravery in facing life's absurdities, of survival without community, ritual, story, fantasy, prayer, or ultimate faith. It is the story of how one can get through a lot with very little, living day to day, sunrise to sunrise, challenge to challenge. To me, her life was a prayer. It was the prayer that says, in the words of Deuteronomy, "I have set before you a blessing and a curse . . . therefore, choose life." She had chosen. She had chosen life, first for her son and then for herself, over and over again. In my view, that was a religious response. For Cary, it was just how she was programmed.

If Beulah, whose story you heard in the last chapter, met Cary, she would tell her that it was God who brought her, in the words of the psalm, "weeping at night and joy in the morning." Cary would not use that language. Cary taught me that the spiritual journey of parenting, while it may be enriched by the tools our traditions offer, is ultimately about the blessings we say with our steps, with our endurance. It is about walking the path to its end with integrity, putting one foot in front of the other. If along the way, we experience the mystery and wonder of it all, that is a bonus. If we believe, as some of us do (at least some of the time) that God plants joy deep within us to well up at the most difficult moments, so be it. But even if we do not, *we still have made the journey*. We still have chosen life.

Nachman of Bratslav, the Hasidic rebbe whose infant son died and whose entire passage through life was a difficult one, explained that "all the world is just a narrow bridge." For him, as for Cary, the heart of the matter was walking fearlessly across that bridge. "The essence," he said, "is not to fear at all."

A wise mother told the author Robert Coles, "Children are souls of God, put here to teach us something while we're trying to teach them something." What children teach us is the truth of the Hillel sandwich. One of the first mothers I interviewed told me that when she was a child in a mostly secular family, the one religious rite that never failed to engage her was the Passover seder. She was especially taken with the tradition of eating a Hillel sandwich, the bitterest horseradish combined with a paste of sweet nuts and fruits. "The taste of that sandwich," she said, "confirmed something that nothing else in my environment even acknowledged—the truth of the connection between sorrow and joy. I always sensed that truth in my heart, but on Passover I got to taste it."

As I was completing this book, I met a beautiful young Israeli woman at a party. When I told her about my topic, she said I must interview her. Had she ever had a spiritual journey in becoming a parent!

I arrived in her simple, well-kept home, flooded with sunshine, natural fabrics, and cool, light colors. Wooden toys were everywhere. Shira was twenty-five, an immigrant with two children, ages two and one. She had come to this country with her husband just four years ago because of his work. The first two years had been wonderful. She had begun to find herself as a dancer. Her decision to become pregnant had been made with deliberation and joy.

"As I prepared for the baby, I realized I had never been so clear in my life. I was totally ready to give everything for this child. My pregnancy was beautiful. I was in heaven. I was dancing less and spending more time working on myself and the growing relationship with my unborn child. I kept a journal, I read books about pregnancy, birth, child care, health, and nutrition. I took good care of my body. Each day I would light a candle, then sit in the bathtub for three hours and meditate. I began a dialogue with the being within me. For the first six months, it was like learning to play the piano, one note at a time. But after that, the dialogue was in good shape. Everyday, we grew closer."

All this sounded wonderful, but as I listened and recorded, I wondered whether it would be useful for my book. It was so perfect. Needless to say, the birth was fabulous, the nursing was exquisite, and the love affair between mother and child was rapturous. By the time we were nearing the child's three-month birthday, I was convinced I had heard enough. Clearly, Shira had been graced with a blessed journey. Would that it could be that way for everyone! I turned off my computer and prepared to pack up and leave.

"Wait!" she said. "This is where the spiritual journey *begins.*" I sat down again, ready to hear the rest of the story.

"I went to my doctor for a checkup when the baby was three months old. I was shocked to learn that I was pregnant again! I was very committed to nursing and still enjoying it immensely. The doctor warned me that nursing throughout a pregnancy and then nursing two children would be very difficult for my body. I was scared but willing to try.

"This pregnancy unfolded as my older child grew to age one. I was always tired, often grumpy, and very hard to live with."

"What about the journal?" I asked.

"No time for that."

"And the meditation?"

Shira laughed. "I was lucky to get five minutes to myself each day. And that was during the pregnancy. By the end, I was very heavy, bleeding a lot. I was still having to pick up and carry my older one. I was terrified of the birth, and it turned out to be very hard. The six months after the birth, however, were much worse. I was physically depleted and emotionally drained. I cried every day. When my husband came home from work, I would make demands on him. I'd threaten to quit! All the black parts of my soul started to come out. Pain from my childhood I had long forgotten was now right there, with me every minute. I found myself so angry that one day my older child looked at me, and I saw fear in his eyes. I knew I had to change.

"When I had half an hour to myself—in the middle of the night after one nursing and before the next—I would lock myself in the bathroom, fill up the bathtub, and talk to myself. Again and again and again. I did this for months. I'd say, 'Your mother and father are across the world. Your husband is working to make a living. You are going to have to find your own inside light to get through the day. You are going to have to rebuild yourself as a person.' It was like learning how to breathe again.

"I never knew anything could be so hard until I had to go through it. Caring for two children under the age of two was so demanding it made me a crazy person for a while. But I believed in what I was doing, and ultimately I came to believe in my light.

"Eventually, by hanging in there and waiting, I did reconnect with Spirit. It was even better than before. It was like a reunion with a long-lost lover. I found out that longing can be good for a relationship."

"So," I concluded, "for you, the spiritual journey of parenting was not the depth of love, the awe of connection, the beauty, the bliss. It was the struggle, the challenge, the strength you found to transcend your own limitations."

"No," she corrected me, "it was *all of it.*"

I thought about the Hillel sandwich—the bitter and the sweet in one mixed-up mouthful. Mary Lou would understand. She was the Catholic widow whom I interviewed, the mother of ten grown children who had a strong and lively faith. Mary Lou had seen it all. "My children have brought me the greatest happiness I've ever known and heartbreak so complete and total that I felt a heavy rock where my soul had been. I remember coming home from having my appendix removed when my oldest son was two. When he saw me coming, he jumped into my arms and pulled me toward him. I could not believe anything could hurt so much and also feel so wonderful *at the same time.* Raising children was the hardest work I ever did in my life, and I would give almost everything I own to be nursing a baby again. I'm old now, and I tell my children what I told myself all through those years of raising them. All I want on my tombstone is two words: She tried."

Here, then, is the true "finding" of all my research. Being a parent is exhausting, miraculous, difficult, awesome, stressful, delightful, terrifying, and growth producing. Yet out of all the noise and confusion, the nights and the mornings and the afternoons, we emerge deeper and wiser than we were when we began. One of the Hebrew names for God is The Place. The Place, I believe, where it all comes together.

During a particularly difficult period in my parenting life, I came across a statement that spoke to me with great power. It said, "Everything that has happened in the past is an illusion. Only the love given and the love received are real." For weeks, I recited that over and over to myself as a mantra. It helped. It reminded me that there had been much love given, much love received. This was at a time when I had been deeming love an illusion and only the mistakes and failures real.

But as I worked on this book, I realized that the statement was actually heretical to both Judaism and Christianity. It was also a heresy in my "parenting faith," as it had grown and developed in conversations with other parents.

It is all real. The walks in the woods. The spit-up. The birthday parties. The nights in the emergency room. The anger at the kids for growing up too slowly, for growing up too quickly, for *never* putting the tops back on the markers. The separations, physical and emotional, premature and long overdue. The drudgery. The exhaustion is real too. And then there is the sheer wonder of it all.

My goal in writing this book was a sense of wholeness for myself, or at least a glimpse of it. Did it work? Actually, there were many such glimpses: as I sat with other parents in conversation, amazed and moved by the texts of their lives; as I sat at home at my computer, searching for the sermon hidden in those texts, humbled by my duty. The refrain that kept going through my mind was "throw away the script."

The child-care books tell parents what to buy before we have children. And rocking chairs *do* help. But what the books fail to tell us is what to get rid of: expectations, assumptions, plans. Over and over, mothers and fathers told me what the spiritual journey of parenting had taught them: to be surprised. Remember Kim, the gay man who adopted a child with his partner of fourteen years? I asked Kim how his father, an aging immigrant who had been schooled in the old ways in China, had reacted. "It was really tough for my father. The mission of a Chinese parent is to raise a son who will produce a biological male heir. Nothing was going according to the plan. I was *adopting* a child, adopting a *girl*, and to top it off, adopting a girl who was not Chinese. But as soon as Linda could speak, I taught her a few Chinese words and we brought her home to my dad. Within an hour, they were happily playing peekaboo on the rug. It certainly was not what my father had thought he wanted, but it was wondrous just the same."

I was in awe of Kim's father and the hundreds of other parents who were my companions these past years. As I thought about their journeys, their triumphs, and their disappointments, their nights and their mornings, they all began to flow into a great stream of unfolding days. I felt respect, acceptance, compassion—not only for other parents but for myself. My own personal parenting themes—hassle, obsessing, guilt—began to subside. Viewing my own journey amongst those of all the other parents gave me perspective, a friendlier, less harsh place from which to judge myself.

But I never did arrive at The Place. In the Prologue, I confessed my secret mall life. Far from spending all my time at places of worship, I spent much of it as a young parent, more than I like to remember, at a temple for the worship of American consumerism, keeping myself going not through prayer but by periodic infusions of sugar. I understood completely when my friend, contemplating a second child, said, "I am worried. I am such a nice person when I am overrested and underworked."

Being a parent *still* leaves me sleepy and off center. The problem is not lack of meaning—I have a whole book about meaning and parenting, and *I wrote it!* Rather, it is the inability to focus. It is death by details, the work and worry that obscure the larger picture. This book was conceived thirteen years ago, as I rocked my first child to sleep. I am sending the final draft to the publisher three days before that same child becomes a Bat Mitzvah. It is taking an enormous effort of will to remember that this event is about a religious transformation and not about who is going to bring the prayer books and who is going to bring the coffeepot.

My friend Judy, who read drafts of this book over a period of a year, said, "When I read your book the first time, I vowed to be more aware of the miracles around me, to become a more sensitive, patient, conscious parent, to transform drudgery into a spiritual challenge. Now, six months later, waking up, meals, baths, bedtimes are still about transitions. And transitions are still 90 percent hassle 90 percent of the time."

Judy and I agreed that The Place is a destination but never a dwelling and that occasional moments of transcendence are all we can really hope for. Maybe I'll have such a moment when I see my daughter read from the Torah on Saturday for the first time. More likely, it will happen tomorrow, while on line at the copy center. Spirituality is not something huge and distant and elusive. Instead, it is tucked within the moments, the ordinary activities of waking, of eating, of going to sleep. Sometimes, we are fortunate enough to notice. Of course, there will always be the other times, when just having made it through the evening without losing it (or being able to start over again *after* losing it) will be an accomplishment.

When I learn how to keep centered not only when preaching parenting but also when practicing it, I will write another book. Until then, I leave you with a story: there was once a devout Christian who had trouble praying. Every time he tried to think about God, his thoughts wandered to images of beautiful women. He went to his priest for guidance. The wise priest advised him not to banish his thoughts but rather to weave them into his prayer. Let him continue thinking about beautiful women and create a prayer around the ideal of beauty as one of God's great achievements.

This is just what we parents can learn to do, if we are lucky. We can let the distraction become part of the worship. A poet I interviewed told of sitting for hours with a poem, unable to figure out how to conclude it. Then, from the next room, she heard her son crying. After singing him back to sleep, she returned to the poem and wrote, "My child cries. I sing to him." Her pen kept moving, and out flowed the ending that had eluded her.

Martin's wife has the same gift for integration. "She incorporates whatever new craziness the children throw her way," Martin told me with awe. "She makes it part of the song of her life." This is the real challenge of our spiritual lives as parents: to take our distracting thoughts, not to mention the distracting nursing, dressing, schoolwork, sibling fights, family vacations, baths, stories, meetings, and bedtimes, and make of them the prayers that are our lives.

Social Work

Oakland, California 95031-6383